DATING SMART

NAVIGATING THE PATH TO MARRIAGE

MENUCHA
PUBLISHERS

ROSIE EINHORN, L.C.S.W. &
SHERRY ZIMMERMAN, J.D., M.SC.

Menucha Publishers, Inc.

© 2013 by Rosie Einhorn and Sherry Zimmerman

Typeset and designed by Beena Sklare

All rights reserved

ISBN 978-1-61465-088-1

Published and distributed by:
Menucha Publishers, Inc.
250 44th Street
Brooklyn, NY 11232
Tel/Fax: 718-232-0856
www.menuchapublishers.com
sales@menuchapublishers.com

Printed in Israel by Chish

Abraham J. Twerski, M.D
1342 Princeton Road
Teaneck, NJ 07666
Tel: (201) 357-5083
Fax:(201) 357-5081
e-mail coby613@aol.com

Family stability and wholesomeness have been the backbone of Jewish survival, and it is no secret that the family is now under great stress. Some of the problems could be eliminated if the basis of the marriage was firmer.

Rosie Einhorn and Sherry Zimmerman bring a wealth of experience and keen judgment to this issue. *Dating Smart* is must reading for all interested in *shidduchim*—the prospective partners, parents, *rabbanim*, and therapists.

HANOCH TELLER
RECHOV YEHOYARIV 4
JERUSALEM 97354 ISRAEL
972 2 823919 Tel
972 2 818149 Fax

Dating Smart is a repository of wisdom and sound advice by a team of experts in the field of *shidduchim*. There isn't much they don't address in this encyclopedic work (certainly nothing I could think of), nor is there an issue that is not awarded cogent and lucid counsel.

For those floundering—if not in fact awash—in a sea of doubt and indecision regarding the most important decision they will every make in their lives, sagacious counsel is not only indicated, it is mandatory. And although there are no shortage of wise and caring individuals, few have anywhere near the expertise or experience that Rosie Einhorn and Sherry Zimmerman have accumulated. For one who is grappling with a dilemma for which they have never had a precedent, *Dating Smart* is a secure and steady boat in choppy seas.

The book is eminently readable and engaging; it is also equally appropriate for those already married. Everyone is—or at least should be—involved in assisting with *shidduchim*. *Dating Smart* will ensure that your involvement is smart, effective, and correct.

Rebbitzen Tziporah Heller

Jerusalem, Israel

I had the opportunity to read *Dating Smart*, the newest book written by Rosie Einhorn and Sherry Zimmerman. It is designed for men and women who wish to do their *hishtadlus* so that they are well prepared for the time that their *bashert* comes along. *Dating Smart* also provides in-depth guidance through the entire dating process that follows.

I have known Rosie Einhorn for many years, and am very familiar with her work and success with *frum* singles, and I have gotten to know Sherry Zimmerman and her work with singles and couples as well. These two women have chosen to share their knowledge, experience, and expertise with a wide audience through the writing of *Dating Smart* and their work with Sasson V'Simcha - The Center for Jewish Marriage, Inc., the non-profit organization they founded to help Jewish singles achieve their goals of happy, stable marriages. It is my hope that many will benefit from their professional and personal wisdom that is expressed in *Dating Smart*, as well as through their ongoing work with single men and women .

May Rosie and Sherry have the *zechus* of continuing to help to build many true Jewish homes for *Klal Yisrael*.

ת"ה נ"י

Tziporah Heller
Yerushalayim
Adar 5773

CONTENTS

ACKNOWLEDGMENTS

FIFTEEN YEARS AGO, WHEN WE FIRST BEGAN TO work together, most people were not aware that many men and women were struggling through the dating process. Since we published our first book, *Talking Tachlis,* and began to present programs on effective dating, work with parents of daters, train mentors and matchmakers, share our methods with fellow therapists, and help communities develop supportive networks for singles, that awareness has grown exponentially.

This book is a tribute to all the people who have helped us along the way—the community activists who shared their ideas with us; organizations that sponsored our programs in North America, Europe, and Israel; the many families who hosted us during our travels; the mentors and matchmakers who selflessly gave their time to help couples come together; and the daters themselves, who have inspired us to continue to devote ourselves to helping more and more Jewish men and women build their *bayis ne'eman b'Yisrael.*

It's hard to single out specific individuals who have been exceptionally helpful to us and our work. We are both indebted to Rabbi Avrohom Czapnik, head of the Jewish Learning Exchange in Los Angeles, who first inspired Rosie to develop a career niche working with single men and women. He's continued to provide advice as well as a forum for many of our programs.

We're indebted to Mrs. Estee Stimler and Mrs. Joanne Dove, who been driving forces behind many *shidduch* initiatives in London and have been invaluable to every aspect of our work. Matchmakers par excellence Mrs. Devorah Felman and Mrs. Heather Sirota have both shared insights that have helped us immeasurably. Rebbetzin Tziporah Heller is a source of spiritual information and always makes herself available to answer any questions we have about all aspects of our work.

This book could not have reached the hands of our readers without the support of Mr. Hirsch Traube and Mrs. Esther Heller of Menucha Publishers, and the excellent skills of our editor, Mrs. Chaya Baila Gavant. Thank you also to Mrs. Beena Sklare for her cover design and typesetting.

Both of us are truly blessed to be able to express our gratitude to Rosie's parents, Rivka and Moshe Loboda, and Sherry's parents, Sylvia and Leonard Scheinberg, may they all live and be well. They've inspired each of us with their love, advice, and living examples of their vibrant marriages.

We could not have been doing this work for so long without the unwavering support of our husbands, Avery

Einhorn and Saul Zimmerman. In addition to enabling us to devote so much effort to running our nonprofit organization Sasson V'Simcha—The Center for Jewish Marriage, they have been at our sides with practical ideas, encouragement, and doses of humor, and their love continually inspires us to help more men and women find the right person so they can have a good marriage. We also thank our children and our children-in-law, many of whom have "entered the family business" by making matches, setting up *shidduch* groups, counseling daters, mentoring, and teaching *chassanim* and *kallos,* for their enthusiasm and well-considered suggestions.

Finally, we have tremendous *hakaras hatov* toward HaKadosh Baruch Hu, who has enabled us to participate in the bringing together of so many Jewish couples as they develop the foundations for their homes and families. His *hashgachah peratis* first enabled us to meet thirty-seven years ago at Rosie and Avery's *sheva berachos,* to become friends and later business partners, and to be able to use the knowledge He has given us to help *klal Yisrael* in such a rewarding way.

INTRODUCTION

PERHAPS YOU ARE TWENTY-EIGHT YEARS OLD AND have been dating for more than seven years. You still haven't met your *bashert* and wonder if you will ever be lucky enough to do so. Everyone tells you, "It's only a matter of time," or "It would be easier if you weren't so picky." You feel a twinge of jealousy every time one of your friends becomes engaged. At every wedding you attend, you hear the well-intentioned, "*Im yirtzeh Hashem* by you."

You may be emotionally drained by the cycle you go through each time you meet a new prospect. Naturally nervous about whether your date will have an agreeable personality and pleasing appearance, you psyche yourself into believing that this will be the right person and the two of you will feel an instant connection. Then comes the disappointment that follows when your evening does not live up to your expectations and you know you must begin the cycle again with yet another *shidduch.*

You may experience both happiness and regret each time you hear of a friend having a new baby, and you feel out of place when you spend Shabbos with your married sister's family. You wonder, *When will I find my bashert? When can I stop pasting a smile on my face each time I hear another person wish me, "Soon it will be your turn"?*

Perhaps you are a thirty-two-year-old *ba'alas teshuvah* who has been religious for the past six years. You have finally convinced your family that you are committed to being observant and that your lifestyle will always be different from the one in which you grew up. Your problem is with dating. Your family and long-time friends don't know men who want the same things out of life as you do. Your circle of *frum* single friends keeps getting smaller as more friends become engaged. You're glad to see them building happy homes, but you wish their husbands knew someone to introduce to you. Not knowing where else to turn, you've started to consult with *shadchanim*. Although some matchmakers have arranged dates for you, you still have not met your *zivug*.

The rational side of you knows that no fairy godmother is hiding in the wings, ready to wave her magic wand and make Prince or Princess Charming appear at the right moment. The emotional side of you agonizes over which combination of prayers, *shiurim*, *shadchanim*, makeovers, and personal enrichment courses will finally work.

What if you could find a tried-and-true formula that would increase your likelihood of finding your future spouse? Wouldn't it be great if you, with the help of Hashem, could be your own fairy godmother, so that the next wedding you celebrate will be yours?

The Talmud teaches us that forty days before a baby is born a voice from Heaven announces Hashem's choice for that baby's future husband or wife (*Sanhedrin* 22a). For many of us, the knowledge that Hashem has selected our *bashert* is small consolation for the disappointment we feel over our single status. We wonder if we will ever be fortunate enough to cross paths with our *zivug*, or if we will be looking in the wrong direction when he or she walks by. How will we know when we have met the right person for us to marry? Will we be able to share a stable, loving relationship with our future husband or wife?

Dating Smart gives single *frum* men and women the skills, knowledge, and clarity that will help them navigate the path to a healthy and enduring marriage. They begin by learning more about themselves and formulating long-lasting goals and ambitions based on their inner needs. With this new understanding, they can determine what truly important qualities to look for in a future spouse and develop reasonable expectations about dating and marriage. They can then move through the dating process with an awareness of how to build the kind of strong, caring relationship that forms the basis of a good marriage.

When we wrote our first book, *Talking Tachlis*, almost fifteen years ago, we were concerned about what we felt was a looming *shidduch* crisis. We saw single men and women floundering through dating, having trouble deciding who was right for them and finding it difficult to build healthy and enduring relationships. Growing numbers of daters were unhappily single for prolonged periods of time and felt frustrated that they couldn't change their situation. Many daters had unreasonable or unrealistic expectations about how dating should progress, what to look for in a marriage partner, and what marriage was about.

Parents and friends of daters who understood the challenges didn't know how to help their children or friends successfully navigate the path to marriage, or how to advise them about reasonable expectations for this process. *Talking Tachlis* presented an effective strategy that daters and the people who cared about them used to achieve their goals of dating successfully for a strong, lasting marriage.

Today, it seems that the numbers of struggling daters and the length of their struggle have increased exponentially. We believe one of the primary reasons for this is that many marriage-minded men and women haven't learned how to optimize the dating process.

One of the ways that all of us learn how to do things is by observing others and modeling ourselves after them. In today's world, it's hard to find role models for the dating process, because in many contemporary circles "courtship" is out of fashion, and because many of the people who are dating are as confused as the next person about how to navigate the path to the wedding canopy. *Dating Smart* can help clear up that confusion and serve as a dater's GPS to his or her ultimate destination.

Many people begin to go out before they have figured out what they should be looking for, how to find potential dating partners, and what criteria to use when deciding if someone is appropriate for them. They often don't know what to expect during the initial stages of dating, how to decide whether to continue beyond that point, and how they can develop an emotional connection and build the relationship. Daters often receive little guidance about recognizing and addressing potential red flags, evaluating whether they and their dating partner are right for each other, and addressing barriers that may keep them from moving a good relationship forward to engagement. The step-by-step approach offered in this book gives daters the tools to deal with each of these stages of the dating process.

We've included here all the strategies we introduced fifteen years ago in *Talking Tachlis* because they have proven to be timeless. These are supplemented with additional guidance based on another decade and a half of our experiences with marriage-minded men and women—and the people who care about them.

The path of dating for marriage hasn't changed since *Talking Tachlis* was first published, but the misconceptions and stumbling blocks that daters grapple with have intensified. *Dating Smart* addresses them as it guides daters through every step of the dating process, beginning with the most important step of all: understanding oneself.

In order to get the maximum benefit from *Dating Smart*, we encourage you to initially read the book through to the end. Then go back and read each chapter more slowly, and do the exercises presented in chapters 1, 6, 7, 8, and 10. Some of these exercises have been designed to help you learn how to be introspective, a skill that will enable you to be more self-aware and to feel more present in your dating, so that you can learn as much about the other person as you can, have the clarity to make good choices, and relate to your dating partner on a deeper level.

The exercises in chapters 6, 7, and 8 are designed to help you address common stumbling blocks that many daters encounter, such as ways of thinking or acting that can keep you from developing a close connection to another person or from looking at your situation with clarity. The questions in chapter 5 can help you evaluate the "rightness" of your relationship after you've been dating each other long enough to be thinking of becoming engaged. Save the "dating vacation" we describe in chapter 9 in the event you feel you've lost your optimism and enthusiasm and want to take a break so you can rejuvenate your feelings and look forward to dating once again.

Although this book is primarily geared for men and women who are dating, it's also a helpful tool for dating mentors and coaches, parents and friends of daters, and anyone trying to make matches. Many younger daters rely extensively on their parents and friends to network on their behalf. Chapters 2 and 3 may be of particular interest to those who are networking for children or friends. We hope that parents and friends of daters read the entire book, and not just these chapters, to gain insight into what daters are experiencing and how you can empathize, support, and guide them through the process.

Writing this book has been a labor of love, drawn on

our personal experience in psychotherapy, family law, mentoring, and mediation. Although many of our vignettes may appear to be aimed at a female readership, this book is intended to be of benefit to both men and women.

All of the vignettes in this book are based on actual case histories, but parts of each of them have been fictionalized to protect the identities of those involved. No description in any vignette matches any actual person.

We hope *Dating Smart* will enable each reader to develop the skills she or he needs to make the dating process easier and more likely to result in success.

Rosie Einhorn and Sherry Zimmerman
February 2013

CHAPTER 1

WHAT TO LOOK FOR

ALL OF US HAVE IDEAS ABOUT WHAT TO LOOK FOR in a prospective spouse. The terms *sensitive, understanding,* and *good sense of humor* are on everyone's list. In addition, each of us expects to meet someone whose religious observance and lifestyle are compatible with our own level of religious commitment, be it a full-time learner, a businessman or professional who sets aside time for learning, or a *ba'al teshuvah* who would be comfortable with our own growth in Yiddishkeit.

If we made *shidduchim* by simply feeding a list into a database that would produce a number of prospective suitors, this list of sought-after qualities would be fine. In reality, though, using a list of general characteristics to find a marriage partner dooms most searches to failure. That's because our search criteria are so broad that we'll hear about any number of "nice" people who are far off the mark for us. We need to be more specific about the qualities we'd like a potential spouse to possess.

But we can't do that until we have a good idea of who we are. And that's where our search for our future mate should start—with understanding ourselves.

Each of us is a composite of life experiences—the way we were brought up, our relationships with our parents and other family members, our education, events that have shaped our personality and worldview, and our hopes and dreams. Sometimes we try to live up to others' expectations about the life we should lead, and we mold our decisions and our dreams for the future on what looks good to others, instead of on what's right for us. Someone embarking on a search for the person she plans to build a life with should be looking for someone who's right for her, not someone who matches other people's expectations. And she has to start with having a good understanding of who she is, what she values, and what she wants out of life.

A good way to acquire this understanding is to set aside quiet, private time to perform a self-evaluation exercise. This is a true *cheshbon hanefesh,* which takes time and introspection.

The *mussar sefer Cheshbon Hanefesh* by Rabbi Mendel of Satanov (Feldheim Publishers, 1995) describes the methodology one can utilize to evaluate his or her personality and improve those characteristics that are not in keeping with good *middos.* The author sets forth thirteen personality traits each individual should strive to improve over a period of time.

It isn't necessary for a prospective dater to change her

basic personality in order to increase her likelihood of finding someone with whom she can build a healthy and happy marriage. Nevertheless, the technique of personal introspection recommended by Rabbi Mendel is useful to anyone who wants to better understand her personality and work on improving those character traits that can help her become a better marriage partner.

The purpose of your self-evaluation is to become clearer about who you are and what you want out of life. It is imperative that you use a notebook to record your thoughts, because you will certainly forget some of them. Ask yourself the following questions, and write down your answers to each of them:

- **What is my current level of religious observance?** Do I want to grow religiously, or am I content to stay where I am? What is my personal commitment to Torah study? Am I satisfied with my level of knowledge and the amount of time I devote to learning?

- **What are my personal talents and character strengths?** Think in broad terms—am I artistic, musical, athletic, a creative thinker? Am I dependable, loyal, determined, intellectual, fun-loving, easy to get along with, compassionate, organized? How do I use these talents and strengths? Do I underutilize any qualities I'd like to develop further?

- **What are my expectations and dreams for myself?** Am I planning to mother a large brood of children and support my husband while he learns in *kollel*, or be active in community organizations? Do I have educational or career objectives, such as obtaining a degree, working in a field I enjoy while raising a family, or starting my own business?

After you've finished writing down your observations about yourself, take some time to go over them. You may want to turn your stream-of-consciousness writing into an orderly list that you can work from.

EVALUATING OR REEVALUATING YOUR GOALS AND DREAMS

Your self-evaluation doesn't end with this first exercise. In order to better understand yourself, your next step is to better understand your short- and long-term goals.

Too many people who are looking for a mate only focus on the goal of getting married instead of looking at what they want to achieve in their own lives and whether the person they marry has compatible personal goals. In addition, very few people look beyond the present when they conduct a self-evaluation. Yet none of us lives a static life; change is part of human nature. We must take into consideration that our needs and ambitions change continually.

The second step in searching within yourself involves going through each entry on the list you've made and trying to envision where you see yourself in a month, in a year, and in five years. Do you see yourself growing spiritually? How do you envision utilizing your creativity, talents, and strengths? Are there any *middos* that you want to improve or develop?

Your projections about these categories are interrelated to the changes you envision about your dreams and goals for the future. As a growing person, your dreams should not be static; throughout your life, you'll accomplish some of them, modify some, and eliminate others. This part of the exercise is your opportunity to decide which of your dreams and goals you've already accomplished, and which you want to change or eliminate either because they are no longer practical or because you've grown beyond them.

You should also consider whether you have any dreams or goals that you would be willing to change or set aside if they wouldn't be beneficial to your relationship with your future spouse. Are there new hopes or ambitions you can consider in their stead? Equally important, do you have dreams or goals that you simply can't abandon or change because your emotional well-being is dependent on them?

Knowing where you can be flexible and where you can't be will help you decide if someone is a good person for you to date. That's why it's important to do this exercise now, rather than after you meet a promising dating partner.

The process of reevaluating your goals can be better understood by looking at what one *ba'alas teshuvah* experienced when she first decided to become religious.

RUTHIE ALWAYS DREAMED OF BEING AN ACTRESS and model. Tall, with dark, classic good looks, she appeared in local dramatic productions as a teenager, and she looked forward to majoring in drama in college. Ruthie's life took a turn when she started to become *frum* in her freshman year. In time she began to keep kosher and attend synagogue on Shabbos. She struggled with the idea of becoming *shomer Shabbos* because it meant that she could no longer appear in plays that were performed on Shabbos.

As Ruthie grew in observance, she realized that the laws of *tznius* precluded her from modeling many modern fashions, and she no longer felt comfortable parading around in what Western culture considered fashionable. But Ruthie couldn't give up her love of the theater, and after much soul-searching she became a high school English and drama teacher who also stages and directs plays and musicals for girls' high schools and women's organizations.

Ahuva's story highlights how this reevaluation can work for a dater.

WHEN AHUVA MOVED TO ISRAEL, SHE FELT AS though she had finally come home. She'd grown up in a city with a small Orthodox community and always hoped to make aliyah with a husband and, perhaps, children. When Ahuva realized that she'd exhausted the pool of eligible daters in her area and might have better luck in a larger Jewish community, she decided to build a life in Jerusalem.

Ahuva loved Israel, and her career in public relations blossomed. However, ten years after her move, Ahuva still hadn't found the right person to marry and raise a family with.

Ahuva had always dated men who, like her, had never been married before. When she turned thirty-five, however, Ahuva decided that it was time to reassess her priorities. She did some serious soul-searching and realized that finding a man she could relate to, love, and admire was more important than his never having been married, not having children, or living in Israel.

"I need someone smart, kind-hearted, put-together, and responsible," she said to herself. "That's what's really important to me. I may not need the packaging I've been looking for up until now."

With that, Ahuva told the matchmakers and friends who had been setting her up that she would consider meeting widowed or divorced men, and would be willing to relocate.

Within a few months, Ahuva had agreed to go out with the man who subsequently became her husband. She's now happily helping him raise his two little boys and the daughter they have together in their home in a large American city.

Soul-searching is a difficult exercise. In order to clarify what's really important to you at this point in your life, you may have to let go of some of the expectations and wishes that were part of you for a long time, as Ahuva did. Sometimes you need to sift through the plans you've made for yourself and ask yourself if that's really what you want, or are you just reflecting what other people have told you you should want.

It can be very tempting to base your plans for the future on what you've been told you "should" do, instead of on what will help you feel fulfilled. In the long term, you're likely to be more satisfied with your life and your marriage if you understand yourself well enough to establish priorities, clarify what you want to achieve, and think of different ways you can pursue your goals both while you're dating and once you find the right person to marry.

CLARIFYING WHAT'S RIGHT FOR YOU

KAYLA FELT THAT SINCE SHE WAS APPROACHING thirty and had not found "the One" after nine years of dating, she had to marry someone who was sensational. She wanted a man who was fairly established in a profession, fun loving, good looking, and from a good family. *Yichus* would be an added bonus, but not absolutely necessary.

As time passed, Kayla's standards got higher. She dated a number of men who met many of her criteria, but each time Kayla realized that someone didn't have them all, she lost interest. Now her ideal mate had to earn a certain salary, live in one of a few clearly defined neighborhoods, and have a certain amount of tangible assets. After all, she had waited this long. How would it look for her to "settle" for someone who didn't meet her criteria?

Kayla's focus on material characteristics and outward appearance is both misguided and unrealistic. Is her potential spouse's address and job description more important to her than integrity, the ability to work toward a goal, and a strong orientation to family and community? Equally important, where are Torah values in Kayla's screenplay?

Kayla would be better off clarifying what she wants in a relationship with her future husband and what kind of personal qualities are important to that relationship. Can she picture herself in a year, after all of the flurried activity of an engagement and wedding is behind her, and she and her future husband are settling down to married life? What kind of a home life does she want? Can she picture them eating breakfast together, talking over the day's events, or sitting at their Shabbos table? Can she see them having a close emotional relationship?

Fast forward another five years. If they're blessed with children, how are they each involved in raising their family, running their home, and providing for material needs? What *middos* can Kayla see herself and her husband teaching their children?

By thinking about the answers to these questions, Kayla will understand herself better and will be more realistic about the type of person with whom she can build a happy married life.

IDENTIFYING WANTS AND NEEDS

Sociology 101 classes often have students chart a society's wants and needs. A similar exercise can help us clarify and prioritize what we're looking for in a marriage partner.

In a sociological sense, *needs* are the basics a society must have to function: shelter, food, water, air, a system of government, and the like. On an individual level, all of us need shelter, food, water, air, and personal safety. Our other needs are more intangible. They are the physical and emotional qualities that must be satisfied for us to feel secure, balanced, and content.

For example, some of us would feel incomplete without a close relationship with our family, while others are satisfied with only casual contact with family members. Some people are insecure about their own abilities and need reassurance from others. There are individuals who must draw, sculpt, write music, or play the piano every day in order to feel whole. Torah learning, too, can be an essential element of someone's sense of being. Many people feel a strong need to give to others and constantly look for ways to involved themselves in *chesed* activities.

When we recognize these needs within ourselves, we simultaneously acknowledge that the person we marry will have to allow these needs to be met, either directly or indirectly. For example, there would be constant marital friction if a *ba'al chesed*'s wife resented the fact that he focused some of his energies outside of their family.

ELIZABETH HAS ALWAYS DESCRIBED HERSELF AS an intellectual. Whether it is a subject in school, a current political issue, or a commentator's discussion on a verse in the parashah, Elizabeth thoroughly analyzes the issue at hand. She wants to fully understand the background of any subject she feels is significant so she can formulate her own opinions.

Elizabeth needs a spouse who will admire her thought processes even though he himself may not be a deep thinker. She, in turn, must be able to understand the manner in which her husband processes information without expecting him to share her intellectual curiosity.

Wants are more superficial than needs; they generally consist of desires that are based more on societal pressures than on items that are essential to our sense of personal wholeness. For example, in the arena of dating, wants could include an insistence that a suitor is taller than you and has a degree from an Ivy League school, or has learned in what you feel is a "top" yeshivah, and you might turn down a suggestion about a great-sounding man who's just your height or who is intelligent and motivated but doesn't have the pedigree you're looking for.

Granted, it's normal and desirable for a person to have wants. All of us are influenced by our environment, and that isn't necessarily a negative circumstance. But when you work at clarifying who you are and what you're looking for in a future spouse, it's important to examine which of your wants reflect what truly makes you feel content, and which of them reflect your image about what your societal influences say your life should be like.

SERENA IS A MOTHER OF TWO AND A PARTNER IN a small law firm. She is happily married to Sam, who never had the desire to attend college and runs a successful carpentry business.

When Serena was in law school, a friend had suggested that she meet a "really great guy" who was a "renaissance man"—learned in Torah and knowledgeable about subjects such as architecture and literature. Serena enjoyed her first date with Sam, and felt she could talk to him for hours. Although Serena had never dated anyone without a degree, when Sam revealed that his post–high school education consisted of yeshivah and a business course for the self-employed, she realized that she was fine with his background.

Some of Serena's law school friends were appalled when they heard Sam was a carpenter. How could Serena, a professional, date a blue-collar worker? Fortunately, Serena was impressed that Sam earned a *parnassah* by doing something he loved, and that he set aside a few hours a day for learning. As she expected, within time Sam's wit and lively personality won over her friends.

PUTTING IT ALL TOGETHER – FOUR PLUS FOUR

If you were to list all of the qualities you felt you needed and wanted in a prospective spouse, you would probably have an unmanageable list. The people who try to set you up will have a hard time comparing the potential dating partners they think of to all of the criteria you've set down. You might also fall into the trap of rejecting suggestions that don't have enough of the qualities you're looking for.

We've found that the most workable list is one that has four descriptive phrases of qualities a single is looking for, accompanied by four descriptive phrases about themselves. This list of "Four Plus Four" gives anyone who tries to set you up a workable set of criteria to begin with.

How can you categorize all the information you've discovered about yourself and what you're looking for into a short, concise description that gives a good picture of what you're like and what you want in a marriage partner?

One way to pare down your list is to study it and number the items on it in order of priority. Then take another look at your wants and decide which of them you can set aside because they aren't really that important in the overall scheme of things. For example, a woman who includes "tall" on her list of wants can ask herself, "Do I feel extremely uncomfortable dating someone who isn't very tall, or have I been conditioned to picture myself looking into the eyes of my husband?"

A man might say to himself, "I keep hearing that a girl should not wear more than a size 6. Honestly, I don't even know what a size 6 means. Isn't it enough for a woman to take care of herself and look nice?"

It may be hard to select the four most important qualities in your description of yourself and the four most important qualities you're looking for in a marriage partner, but you'll be able to do it. Next, develop a brief description that includes where you are in life, where you see yourself in the near future, four personal qualities that tell a lot about who you are, and four traits you'd like your spouse to have. It should take you no more than ninety seconds to say.

THE ELEVATOR PITCH

Visualize a midlevel employee in a large company getting on an elevator with the CEO and using their ride from the first to the twenty-third floor executive offices to pitch an idea he's developed. This is called an "elevator pitch," and it has to be interesting and short enough to pique the CEO's interest and get him to invite the employee to discuss it further. Your statement should be able to attract the listener's attention so that he or she says, "I may know someone who'll be a good match."

Here's an example of a description that helped Yitzi meet Eliana. "My son, Yitzi, is twenty-seven and works in the marketing department of a pharmaceutical firm. He just finished his first year of an MBA program. Yitzi davens in a Young Israel–type minyan, learns *daf yomi*, and doesn't watch television. He loves to play baseball and is in a company baseball league. Yitzi is a focused and responsible person, likes to help his family and his neighbors, is neat and well-organized, and has a friendly personality. He's looking for a young woman in her twenties who is intelligent, already knows what she wants in life, thinks family ties are very important, and has a lot of energy."

The elevator pitch is meant to get the next person thinking about whether someone they know might be a good match. Chapter 2, "Making Networking Work," will describe how to use Four Plus Four and the elevator pitch as networking tools.

A POINT OF REFERENCE

Think for a moment about all you've accomplished by performing the exercises in this chapter. You've become more aware of who you really are, and may have determined which qualities you previously believed were important are not essential to having a fulfilling life. You've distinguished between qualities that are more important and less important in your search for the person you'd like to marry.

The knowledge you've developed and the introduction you'll use provides you with a beginning point of reference. It will leave you open to meeting people whom you otherwise would not have considered and will also help you filter out suggestions of people who are clearly not right for you.

Later chapters of this book will explore a number of other considerations that can help you decide which person is the right one for you to marry.

SOME INFORMATION YOU SHOULD KNOW ABOUT YOURSELF BEFORE STARTING TO DATE

. . . .

- The direction in which you'd like your life to go over the next six months, one year, and five years.

- Your personal *hashkafah* and where you see yourself growing over time.

- Your comfort zone for dating someone who is stronger or weaker than you in these areas.

- What kind of living standard you expect to have in the first few years of your marriage, after five years, and long term.

- How you envision Shabbos in your married home. Think in terms of frequent or occasional guests, personal and family time, inviting people you don't know for *kiruv* opportunities, lavish or simple meals, *zemiros*, *divrei Torah*, child-oriented activities, time together as a couple, attending *shiurim*, time to rest and recharge batteries, and board games with the family.

- How flexible you are in all of these areas.

Chapter 2

MAKING NETWORKING WORK FOR YOU

WHAT DO YOU DO WITH WHAT YOU'VE LEARNED about yourself and the qualities you're looking for in a future husband or wife? You use the elevator pitch as a brief introduction describing who you are and what you're looking for. Ideally, a person who hears your description and believes she knows a potential match for you can then ask questions and exchange information to see if the idea has enough merit to present it to both sides.

The process of contacting others to present basic information is called "networking," and it can be done by parents, relatives, friends, and the dater herself. Many segments of the Orthodox community have been networking for *shidduchim* for generations, and it's the way most singles get *shidduch* introductions. Let's take a look at the most effective ways to network.

USING A BUSINESS MODEL

One way to understand networking is to examine where it's used effectively. Although most successful businesspeople and professionals use advertisements and word of mouth to help them build a strong client base and a good reputation, they know that networking can be even more effective. They devote a lot of effort into developing a network of individuals and businesses that can refer clients their way.

Networking is one of the most effective ways for singles to enlarge their social circles and be introduced to suitable people they would never have an opportunity to meet on their own. The majority of married couples say they got together because someone they knew made an introduction or set them up on a blind date.

The problem is that many families don't build a broad enough network and don't give specific enough information that can be helpful to the person they're speaking with. "She's looking for a nice boy with good *middos* who's going to learn as long as possible" can define hundreds of young men, and at the same time defines none of them.

There are many people who should be networking but aren't—these can be parents who aren't used to the concept of actively helping their adult children or singles who don't network on their own behalf. Instead of proactively asking others to help them in their search for the right person, they hope that someone they know will think of them in the future, or they go to a few singles' events in the hopes that they'll be lucky enough to meet a great person.

Daters and their families can learn from business models. Just as businesspeople rely on a variety of resources to achieve success, singles and their families should use every appropriate avenue that will lead them to their future marriage partner, especially networking.

Every social event can be viewed as a networking opportunity for a child or for oneself, whether it's a N'shei supperette, a Shabbos afternoon *shiur*, a Shabbos meal with friends, or a *simchah.* You can turn a date with a good person who's not for you into a networking opportunity for your roommate or best friend. Even a trip to the supermarket can turn into a networking opportunity.

LONNIE PULLED HER SHOPPING CART INTO THE checkout line. No sooner had she maneuvered it behind the customer in front of her that she heard, "Lonnie, I don't believe it. I haven't seen you in ages!" The voice came from her former neighbor, Deena, who'd moved to New Jersey two years before.

"Deena, it's so great to see you. How's everything?"

Lonnie's oldest daughter, Rivka, had recently begun to date. She realized that Deena, whose son was two years older than Rivka, could know some young men who might be good for her. "Deena, you might have some ideas for my daughter, Rivka. Remember how she and your Dovid used to play together when they were little?"

"I can't believe Rivka's old enough to be dating," said Deena. "What's she looking for?"

"Rivka would like a boy who'll start off learning but then go to school and work. It's important for him to be family oriented—close to his own family and to hers. She wants someone who thinks for himself instead of blindly following others, but who knows the importance of having a *rav* to consult with. Rivka isn't materialistic, but she wants someone who understands what it will take to provide for a family with a middle-class lifestyle. And she'd prefer a boy who has an outgoing personality.

"Rivka's a hard worker, yet she likes to take breaks and have fun. She's goal-oriented and accomplishes what she sets out to do. She's very practical, and she wants to work part-time while she raises her family. She sees marriage as a real partnership."

"I'm thinking…I'm thinking," said Deena. "Lonnie, I'm going to write this down when I get home and try to think of a couple of ideas."

Deena telephoned Lonnie about six weeks later to suggest that Rivka go out with a friend of her son's. "You gave me enough information to really understand the kind of boy Rivka wants to meet and to describe her to the other side. He's already said yes. Let me tell you about him…"

The trick is knowing how to network properly—letting people know what you're like, what you're looking for, how they can find out more information, and how they can get in touch with you to discuss an introduction. You may have to educate people who are new to networking about how they can be helpful, and tactfully encourage them to work on your behalf. You'll also have to periodically touch base with the members of your network, as well as look for new venues for networking.

NETWORKING HOW-TO'S

Here are some pointers that can help you network effectively:

- **Compile a list of potential contacts for your network.** Think about including extended family; relatives' relatives; close and not-so-close friends; people you've lost touch with; current and former teachers and rabbis; neighbors; coworkers; and people from your synagogue, classes, and community activities. You can gradually also add others who seem to be good resources—local merchants, customers, and friends of friends. You can also find a few professional *shadchanim* you feel comfortable with and include them in your network.

- **Ask three or four people you know well and respect for their good judgment and integrity to be your references.** These are the people to be called when a prospective date wants to "check you out." Be sure that at least one reference has known you for a long time, even if you haven't been in close contact recently. (This is even true if you are newly *frum*.)

  Talk to each reference about where you are in life, how you have grown and matured, your goals and how you hope to achieve them, the kind of family you would like to have, the qualities you are looking for, your own personal strengths, and what you believe you can contribute to a marriage.

If you have problematic areas of your background, it's better that your reference knows how to discuss them in a positive but honest way. Talk to them about how you overcame and learned from these challenges and how you'd prefer they talk about the subject.

- **Begin to approach the people in your network.** This may feel awkward at first, but it will get easier over time. You can open with this: "I have a special favor I'd like to ask of you. My daughter is dating, and I'm trying to help her find the right person. Can I tell you a little about her and what she's looking for?" Then use your elevator pitch to open up the subject.

- **Take the next step.** If the person you approach has an idea, exchange more information. Don't be shy about telephoning the other side to ask questions. And remember that even if the person you approach doesn't have an idea at the moment, she may have one in the future. Let her know that you'd like to call or e-mail her from time to time to see if she has any new ideas.

Many people get a burst of inspiration but neglect to follow up and then forget the person's idea. Your telephone call every month or two might jog the person's memory.

- **Talk to everyone who may be helpful.** Give them your name and telephone number, so they can be in touch with you in the future. If someone says they think they know of someone, ask when you can call to get more information, and then make the call. Don't wait for them to follow up—they may have the best intentions but forget to do so.

◆ **Show *hakaras hatov* to anyone who suggests an idea.** The suggestion may be from left field, may tell you the other person needs a better idea of what you're looking for, or contains so little information that it's useless—or it may be right in the ballpark. It doesn't matter. Thank the would-be-matchmaker for thinking of you, working hard to find out details, and making the suggestion.

If the idea sounds interesting, specify the additional details you'll need to know before deciding to accept it. If you have to turn down the offer, politely explain that there are a few reasons why it doesn't sound right for you. Ask the person to keep you in mind for the future, and clarify some points that can help them fine-tune their efforts the next time they have an idea for you.

NETWORKING DON'TS

◆ **Network from a positive perspective, not a negative one.** How many times have you heard something like, "My neighbor's daughter is such nice girl but *nebach,* she needs a *shidduch*. At thirty-two, she doesn't have much time left"? Would you or your son want to hear more details about someone who is portrayed as a *nebach?*

◆ **Don't make a suggestion that's too vague to be**

helpful, or has no contact information. "I heard about this *bachur* in the Mir named Gadi… I think his family name is Schwartz, I'm not sure. Maybe he's good for your Sorale. He's twenty-five, got an accounting degree, then decided to learn in Israel for a few years. He's coming back this summer. No, I don't know what town he's from… No, I don't know what he's looking for… No, I don't know if he's going to keep learning or start working. Your nephew learned in the Mir a few years ago…maybe he knows him."

◆ **If you mention a single, follow through with the idea.** It's not helpful to say to your friend, "My niece Chaya is already thirty! We must find her someone." Your friend's answer will probably be, "*Oy*, we really must," and that's the end of the conversation. Instead, describe your niece in a positive light and ask your friend if she can help you think of *shidduch* ideas for her.

NETWORKING FOR THE BA'AL TESHUVAH

Networking can be a challenge for *ba'alei teshuvah* because they usually don't have family members or long-time friends who can relate to their lifestyle. That means that if you are relatively new to *frumkeit*, you have to work harder to build a network.

The first people you should approach for support are your mentors—those who influenced you to become *frum*, the *rabbanim* and teachers who helped you on your journey, and your current *rav* or *rebbetzin*. Don't be reluctant to get in touch with someone who was helpful to you in the past, even if you may have lost contact over time. Most people are happy to hear how you've developed and would love to help you find a *shidduch* if they can.

Other people in your network should be your *frum* friends, members of your shul, and families who host you for Shabbos meals. Find out if the seminary or yeshivah you attended has a matchmaker for alumni and current students, or knows of someone who might be helpful to you. And consider meeting one or two *shadchanim* who specialize in working with *ba'alei teshuvah*.

INTERNET DATING

Another networking tool that has helped daters is matchmaking websites specifically designed for *frum* singles. See appendix B, "Networking via the Web," for more information.

NETWORKING POINTS FOR BA'ALEI TESHUVAH

- Your best reference may be someone who's unfamiliar with shidduch dating. You'll need to explain the *shidduch* process, why people do research, and the type of questions they ask. Bring them up to date about your plans for the future and what you're looking for.

- There may certain issues in your background that you feel uncomfortable about, such as intermarried relatives or lifestyle choices before you became *frum*. Ask your reference to answer questions about these areas in a way that emphasizes the positive. Describe where you are today and how you've moved beyond your past.

- Find a more experienced person show you the ropes, such as a mentor or a married friend who's been through this process. It's a good idea to have a *rav* you connect to who can answer your halachic and hashkafic questions.

- Develop reasonable expectations about the kind of person who is good for you. Don't take it personally if you are rejected for having relatives who aren't *frum*. The right person for you will appreciate you for who you are.

CHAPTER 3

CHECKING OUT A SHIDDUCH

WHEN JEWS LIVED IN SMALL COMMUNITIES IN which everyone knew their neighbors, *shidduchim* were not accompanied by a background check. Today, few of us marry someone who grew up under the caring eyes of our neighbors or relatives. A *yeshivah bachur* may recommend to his wife's friend a *chavrusa* whom he knows only inside the *beis midrash*. A *shadchan* may believe the person he recommends is a lovely young woman without having firsthand knowledge of her *middos* or her past. A well-intentioned uncle may arrange a nephew's first date while deliberately hiding a serious condition such as an emotional disturbance, believing that marriage is all the young man needs to "calm him down."

Knowledge is a critical factor for all daters, no matter their level of religious observance. No one wants to prepare for a first date only to discover that the people who arranged the introduction didn't have correct information...and that they and their dating partner are so different from each other that their evening has turned into a discouraging waste of time.

Daters can avoid these scenarios by finding out more information before deciding whether to accept a promising dating suggestion. We want to know if the person is a good potential partner for us—that they have a similar *hashkafah* and basic values similar to our own, are moving in the same direction in life, come from a background we're comfortable with, possess many of the qualities we feel are important, and are capable of building a healthy marriage. In order to find out this information, we have to ask questions.

Someone who's not familiar with the idea of pre-screening may ask, "Can't I wait for the first date to ask these questions? Why spend hours checking someone out when I could learn everything in one date?"

Yes, you can wait for the date to start asking questions, but unless you're extremely fortunate, this approach can quickly lead to frustration. One person's values or goals clash with your own, the next one lacks maturity or emotional stability, another wants someone with a different level of education or career orientation than you, and one isn't ready to start thinking about marriage for another few years. After a while, you begin to wonder why you didn't check things out more carefully before you said yes.

Dating for marriage is an inherently goal-oriented process, and families of most young people from traditional and *yeshivish* backgrounds understand that it doesn't make sense to go on even a first date with someone who doesn't have most of the qualities their son or daughter is looking for. That's why these families, or the singles themselves, customarily look into details about a prospective *shidduch* or find out more detailed information about a dating partner's background when a relationship begins to get serious. It's a good practice for all marriage-oriented daters to follow.

WHOM TO ASK

Start with the person who made the suggestion and move on from there. Always ascertain how well the person you are speaking to, even the matchmaker, knows the *shidduch* suggestion, how long they've known each other, and in what capacity. Ask anyone who doesn't have a strong connection to your potential date to suggest someone who knows him better.

Try to talk to at least two people who know the potential dating partner through different frames of reference. This can include one person who's known him for a long time (including a friend from a recent *ba'al teshuvah*'s earlier life). Strive to speak to someone who knows the prospective date well. For example, instead of a *rosh yeshivah* or a high school principal, it might be better to talk to a young person's rebbe, seminary teacher, *mashgiach*, counselor, or roommate. For a more established person, consider talking to his community rabbi and/or *rebbetzin*, room-mates, a current friend, or a long-time friend or neighbor.

WHAT TO ASK

Before you ask any questions, it's a good idea to familiarize yourself with the laws of *lashon hara* and *rechilus* as they relate to making inquiries about a prospective *shidduch*. *Guard Your Tongue,* by Rabbi Zelig Pliskin (Gross Bros., 1975), provides an overview of the extent to which one may inquire about a prospective *shidduch,* as well as the nature and amount of information that may be disclosed. The Chofetz Chaim Heritage Foundation has developed materials on this subject that are provided for a nominal fee. (See appendix A for contact information.) Your *rav,* rebbe, or seminary teacher can also provide you with guidance on this subject.

Your initial questions should center around four themes:

1. How accurate is the information I've already been given about this person?

2. What other information do I need to see if he or she is in the ballpark—in terms of *hashkafah,* values, expectations, short- and long-term goals, and character traits?

3. What basic facts do I want to know about this person's background, biography, and emotional state?

4. What is this person looking for in a marriage partner? Do I seem to fit those expectations?

Many people are content to ask a number of basic questions. They're looking for enough answers to indicate that the suggested dating partner is emotionally stable and is in the ballpark. Others will add questions that cover topics that are particularly important to them but may not be important to someone else. People who come from communities in which the dating process is telescoped into a relatively short period of time may ask for a lot of information that other couples expect to learn about over the course of a longer courtship. Choose the method that you feel most comfortable with and go with it.

Sometimes the person making the inquiry is uncomfortable asking questions that center on a potential date's emotional state, his way of relating to his family, or other sensitive areas. These questions sound intrusive, but they have to be asked. Unfortunately, there are people out there who have serious mental illness, hidden drug addiction, alcoholism, severe indebtedness, a sociopathic personality, or financial abandonment of a prior family. An individual who is anxious to get married, or whose family wants to see him find his *bashert*, may intentionally hide these problems from a *shadchan* or a *rosh yeshivah* as they pursue marriage prospects. The *shadchan* has no obligation to investigate whether they exist, and the same can be true of a friend, neighbor, or *chavrusa* who suggests such a person for a *shidduch*. In many cases, this vital information can be discovered with a few well-placed telephone calls to the right people.

You'll find out more information if you ask questions that require narrative answers, meaning the references have to explain rather than reply "yes" or "no." Pointed questions will save you from the following scenario: "Is Meir a nice boy?" "Of course, he's a very nice boy."

This exchange is useless. You can learn much more by asking questions such as, "Can you tell me how he gets along with the boys he rooms with?" "What is his relationship with the other children in his family?" "Can you give me examples of how he does *chesed*?"

PRIMING YOUR OWN REFERENCES

Most daters will provide a short list of references and their contact information. Many references are honest and forthcoming, and will provide someone making an inquiry with all of the information they'll need to make an informed decision about a suggested *shidduch*. Nevertheless, it's important to make sure your references are willing to take time to answer questions about you, have current information, can express themselves clearly, and demonstrate good judgment and integrity.

SAM WAS HAPPY TO GIVE THE SHADCHAN THE name and telephone number of his former high school principal, whom he looked up to as a mentor now, ten years after he finished high school. But even though Sam and the principal saw each other from time to time, Sam had never discussed being a reference with his mentor.

Sam certainly didn't anticipate that the young woman who'd been suggested for him would call the *shadchan* to say, "Tell Sam to get a new reference."

It seems that Sam's mentor had responded to her inquiries with, "You're thinking of dating Sam? I like Sam, but he really needs a good woman to put his head on straight." Sam burst out laughing when he heard the story, saying, "I'm sure he was trying to be funny. And he probably thinks a little bit about it is true." Yet Sam understood that the woman had turned him down because "no normal woman wants to have to put a man's head on straight," and decided to use another person as a future reference.

It's a good idea for your list of references to include at least one person who has known you for a long time, and one person who knows you well now. Update your references on what's been going on in your life—your goals, how you hope to achieve them, the values that are important to you, and your character strengths. Your references will be asked more questions than your "elevator pitch" will cover, so be satisfied that they have a good understanding of your background, who you are, and what you're looking for.

In addition, if there are issues that need to be explained, discuss how you would like your reference to handle questions about it, especially how you overcame challenges arising from a difficult period in your life.

TIPS FOR BA'ALEI TESHUVAH

B*a'alei teshuvah* often wonder how they can suggest a reference who has known them a long time when their long-time friends are unfamiliar with *shidduch* dating. Potential dating partners often want to talk to a reference who has a strong connection with you and knows a lot about your character and background. It may take a while for you to explain the *shidduch* process to an old friend who is not *frum,* but they may turn out to be a valuable resource.

If you are newly religious or from a more modern background, you may be tempted to skip the checking-out process because you don't have relatives to help or are unsure of the correct procedure to follow. It's likely, however, that there are people in your network who can explain the process in more detail, and can even help make inquiries. Even though it may be challenging, checking out prospects is a must for *ba'alei teshuvah,* who are usually set up with other newly *frum* people and would benefit from knowing more details about each other's backgrounds and experiences before deciding to date.

The shortened dating period for *frum* singles is another reason for *ba'alei teshuvah* to make the appropriate inquiries about prospective *shidduchim.* Sometimes, friends and mentors will encourage a new *ba'al teshuvah* to get engaged after a brief period of dating without realizing that he or she probably didn't benefit from the extensive investigations that long-established *frum* families generally conduct. These efforts to help a friend build a *bayis ne'eman b'Yisrael* can end in disaster if the other person has serious problems that could have been disclosed by a more thorough inquiry and/or a longer dating period.

SHARONA LIVED IN ISRAEL HER WHOLE LIFE AND was finishing her degree in mathematics at an Israeli university when she was introduced to Elliot, a twenty-five-year-old American who had come to Israel to learn after he finished college. Sharona and Elliot dated for a few months, and Sharona even met Elliot's sister, who had made aliyah a few years earlier.

Sharona's parents had died a few years earlier, so she lacked the guidance of her own family. She and Elliot became engaged before she had an opportunity to meet other members of Elliot's family, many of his friends, and the rabbi of his shul in America.

Several months after their wedding, Elliot began to miss morning *seder* and eventually stopped going to yeshivah altogether. He lost his appetite and slept a great deal. Sharona believed Elliot showed signs of depression and insisted that he see a psychologist. When Elliot refused, Sharona tried to enlist the help of his sister.

It was then that Elliot's sister confessed that he had been diagnosed with bipolar disorder six years earlier. He went through extended periods in which he refused to take the medication that could control his condition. Sharona also learned that Elliot had not finished college because of his illness. His parents hid his condition from his *mashgiach* as well as from Sharona because they believed marriage was the safety net Elliot needed to force him to take his medication and resume therapy.

By now, Sharona was several months pregnant, and since the couple loved each other, they were determined to work together to monitor Elliot's medication and see that he resumed therapy. Unfortunately,

Elliot's cooperation was erratic, and Sharona suffered from the emotional and financial strain of living with a bipolar spouse until she finally decided to get a divorce. Sharona learned a hard lesson that could have been avoided had she researched Elliot's background before they dated.

Many people will confine their research to two or three well-informed references who sound honest and sincere. Other people, however, say, "If I get the information and answers I am looking for from one or two people, that's enough for me. But if I don't, then I'll make a lot of phone calls."

A lot of indiscriminate phone calls can lead to problems—with people who offer information even though they don't have all of the facts, have a grudge against you or your family, or are not interested in taking enough time to speak on your behalf. Which leads us to our next topic: how to handle negative information.

HANDLING NEGATIVE INFORMATION

Checking out a potential dating partner isn't a hunt for negative information. If you hear something negative, don't rush to pass judgment. You may have spoken to someone with an opinion of the person or their family that no one else shares. Or you may have been told incomplete information by someone who doesn't know the person or the situation well. (It's also possible that they have an unrealistically optimistic view of your potential dating partner or are purposely withholding unfavorable information.) That's why it's a good idea to speak to at least two people, especially if you hear or sense something negative.

Furthermore, if you're not sure what the person you are "interviewing" means to say, or if you need clarification, ask additional, pointed questions. You don't want to reject or accept someone based on incomplete or misunderstood information.

Factor in all of the reliable information you hear, both positive and negative, before making a decision to accept or turn down a dating offer. For instance, you may not be comfortable with the *hashkafah* of the family of a young man who seems to have a lot of qualities you're looking for. Or he may have had a difficult upbringing, was once a little wild, lacked focus, or went off the *derech.*

Instead of automatically dismissing the suggestion because his background concerns you, ask more questions. These can include if and how he's dealt with challenges, if he received therapy or other help from a third party, how he's grown and matured, how he relates to his family members, what direction he's chosen in life, and the ways he seems capable of being a stable, kind, and loving spouse and parent.

AREAS OF CONCERN

If the person you're asking about has had more recent challenges, or has a history of drug or alcohol abuse or serious emotional difficulties, be especially thorough in your investigation. You don't want to unfairly stigmatize someone who can be a healthy partner in a stable marriage, but you also don't want to ignore a serious problem. For example, you may learn that the emotional issues are being successfully managed with therapy and/or medication or were the result of a painful, temporary situation such as the death of a close relative and have been resolved. Or it may be that this person hasn't received help for his condition, isn't cooperating with treatment, or denies there is a problem, and may not be good marriage material.

Here are some areas to be concerned about when you look into the history of a potential *shidduch*:

- **Substance abuse or addiction:** Anyone who currently abuses alcohol or drugs or struggles with addiction is not a good candidate for marriage. A recovering addict who is now sober and in treatment may be a good marriage partner, provided he or she is committed to remain in a twelve-step rehabilitation program, such as Alcoholics Anonymous, for the rest of his life.

  If you're considering someone with a history of addiction or substance abuse, learn more about the challenges they may face because of their condition, as well as how they handle their personal challenges. Don't assume that they can succeed in overcoming their addiction simply because they are *frum* or have "found" Torah. Like everyone else with their background, they will face the challenges of recovery on a daily basis, and they stand the best chance of succeeding if they remain in a twelve-step program.

- **Significant medical conditions:** Some people don't

feel it's necessary to know if their dating partner has a significant medical condition, reasoning that all of us develop conditions as we age. Yet there's no comparison between a person's willingness to deal with the illness of someone they're just getting to know and their ability to do so when a beloved spouse is diagnosed with a life-changing condition. That's why our *rabbanim* tell us that daters with a significant physical or mental health condition must disclose it to a serious dating partner, so that they can take it into consideration when they make a decision about marriage.

Each person's situation is different, and it's vital for daters who have a medical or mental condition to ask a competent *rav* if they must disclose it to a dating partner, and if so, at what point in the dating process. The *rav* may advise a dater to disclose the condition after the couple has begun to relate to each other, because at that point the dating partner will be more open to hearing and processing the information. Sometimes the *rav* will advise disclosure before the couple agrees to go out, and some conditions don't have to be disclosed at all.

It's vital that a dater who has to disclose medical information do so in a positive, matter-of-fact way. Here's how Yonina explained her situation to Bentzi on her fourth date:

ASKED DA'AS TORAH ABOUT WHEN I SHOULD DIScuss something important with a person I'm going out with and was told to do it at this point in the dating. *Baruch Hashem*, I am living a very full life and I feel good. I am also managing a medical condition called diabetes. It means that my pancreas doesn't produce enough insulin to process the sugars contained in the food that I eat, and I have to watch my diet and use an insulin pump to provide what I can't make on my own. If you have any questions about diabetes or how it affects me, I'll try to answer them."

Bentzi did ask a number of questions, and found out more information about diabetes on his own. When he decided to marry Yonina, this was one of the many factors he considered before deciding that she was the right woman for him.

There's nothing wrong with asking questions about a prospective date's medical situation before deciding whether or not to accept a *shidduch* suggestion. "Do you know if he's currently being treated for a medical or emotional condition, or has had one in the past?" is often asked during the checking-out process.

If the answer is positive, we suggest keeping an open mind while asking more questions. Find out about how this person lives his life while managing his condition, how it may impact his long-term health, and the likelihood it may be passed on to his children. This should be one of the many pieces of information you consider before deciding if you'd like to go on a first date.

◆ **Mental illness and personality disorders:** The very words *mental illness* may tempt many daters to run in the other direction. They automatically imagine someone who is unstable and incapable of being in a long-term, mutually giving relationship. Fortunately, many types of mental illness are treated successfully, and once they are recovered former patients are able to lead happy, productive, and emotionally stable lives and have successful marriages. That's why someone who learns that a prospective dating partner was treated for depression, anxiety, obsessive-compulsive disorder, or other conditions should find out detailed information before deciding for or against the suggestion. The person may turn out to be a good candidate for marriage.

However, certain mental illnesses and many personality disorders may affect the patient so severely that he or she is an unsuitable candidate for a long-term relationship. This can be the case with many individuals who have schizophrenia, bipolar disorder, or certain personality disorders and have not responded well enough to medication or treatment to be able to function in a relationship. Sometimes a person who has a serious mental condition may be able to mask it for a while, and actually be pleasant and well-functioning for a few dates, but in time will display behaviors that indicate that something is just not right.

Often people who are well-acquainted with someone who is mentally ill or has a personality disorder are aware that there is a serious problem. It's important to ask if a reference for a suggested *shidduch* knows whether the person in question has ever been treated for mental illness or a personality disorder, displays excessive anger, or seems unstable. Request more information that can help you understand the *shidduch's* true situation.

Bear in mind that this is a sensitive area for many, and the individual you ask may not have detailed information or may actually lie so that you'll give the other person a chance. If you have a sense that a reference is hiding something, or if they give evasive answers, you may have good reason to turn down the suggestion.

◆ **Controlling or abusive personalities:** It's an unfortunate fact that emotional and physical abuse and excessive control sometimes occurs in *frum* families. Sometimes, the first signs that an individual may be inclined toward these behaviors emerge while a couple is dating or after their engagement. That's why organizations such as the Shalom Task Force (see appendix A) provide educational information about signs of potential problems in this area and present assemblies in high schools to teach young women the signs of healthy and unhealthy personality traits and relationships. All daters, regardless of gender, should know this information before they begin dating and should have someone with whom they can discuss questions that may arise during a courtship.

There are also a number of questions that can be asked during the checking-out process to detect warning signs of future trouble. These include questions about how someone handles stressful situations, if he has a *rav* or other authority figure he looks to for advice, whether he has had serious arguments or physical altercations with others, how critical he is, and whether he has a history of control or abuse.

- **Additional areas of concern:** There are a number of other circumstances that may not emerge during the checking-out process, but which a dater should disclose once a courtship becomes serious. While they may not have a bearing on an individual's ability to be a good husband or wife, they will have an effect on a future marriage and have to be discussed before a couple decides to get engaged. These include a prior criminal record, a previous marriage (with or without children), a financial commitment to parents or other family members, preexisting child support or alimony obligations, pending lawsuits, significant personal debt, and bankruptcy.

GENETIC SCREENING

Genetic screening is a vital part of the checking-out process. Hospitals such as Hadassah Hospital in Israel and Einstein Medical Center in Philadelphia have testing programs for individuals and couples. Many people participate in the Dor Yesharim program, which screens potential dating partners for genetic compatibility for marriage. An individual's blood is tested to see if they carry genes for a number of untreatable genetic diseases that are common among Jews. Each participant receives a confidential ID number but does not learn the results of the testing.

When a man and woman want to start dating, or if they are already dating, they call the organization, give their ID numbers, and are advised if they are compatible for marriage or if they both carry a recessive gene for the same disease. Since two carriers of the same disease have a 25 percent chance that their child will be born with the illness in each pregnancy, people who both carry the disease gene usually decide not to begin dating each other or to end their current courtship. They can also obtain genetic counseling.

For more information, contact Dor Yesharim via the information listed in appendix A.

TIPS FOR CHECKING OUT POTENTIAL SHIDDUCHIM

These questions will help you learn the information you need to decide about a *shidduch* suggestion. Phrase the questions so you'll get narrative answers, and ask for explanations or examples to vague, guarded, or unclear answers. You may have to ask, "Is there anyone who knows the situation better and can give me more information?"

◆ How long have you known this person, and how are you connected to each other?

◆ Where did she grow up?

◆ What is his family like? How do the parents get along with each other (even if they are divorced)?

◆ What kind of relationship does she have with her parents?

◆ What are the children in the family like? What kind of relationship do they have with their parents? With each other?

◆ What kind of connection do his parents have with their community? Who is their rabbi? What synagogue do they attend?

◆ What are the parents' education and careers? Their cultural background? Their *hashkafah*?

◆ Where did the person attend school/yeshivah/seminary/college?

◆ What's her *hashkafah* and what direction does she want it to take in the future?

- What role does learning play in this person's life now and in his expectations for the foreseeable future?

- What is her outlook on life?

- What are his personal goals for career, education, and involvement in the community, and how does he hope to achieve them?

- What lifestyle would she like to have?

- How does he like to have fun?

- What are her friends like?

- Does he smoke?

- What is he like on Purim? Simchas Torah?

- How would you describe her dependability? Level of independence? Flexibility? Can she take charge of a situation? In what ways?

- Have you ever seen him deal with an emergency or crisis? How did he react?

- What importance does she place on dressing fashionably? What standards of *tznius* are important to her?

- Do you think he has the emotional stability to be a good marriage partner? What do you base this on?

- What is she looking for in a future spouse?

- Why do you think he would be a good match for me/ my child?

CHAPTER 4

. . . .

THE DATING PROCESS

. . . .

NOT SO LONG AGO, PEOPLE LEARNED NEW SKILLS by observing someone who had experience and then trying it themselves. They learned how to run a business by working in a starting position and watching how their father, uncle, or supervisor did things. They learned a trade by apprenticing to a master in the field, learned to drive after a few frustrating sessions with one of their parents, and learned how to date by watching their friends or older siblings.

Life has gotten a lot more complicated. Today, we go to school to learn business skills or how to work at a trade, and we take driving lessons from a driving instructor. But most of us still pick up our dating skills from watching our friends and older siblings.

When it works—and for many people it does work—it's because we had a workable model to emulate. Many times, though, some of the people whose dating techniques we are observing are having just as hard a time as we are. The dating process has become very confusing, largely because, like everything else in contemporary culture, life has gotten a lot more complicated. We hear so many conflicting messages about what we should think and feel that we don't have a clear model for dating that builds a relationship which can lead to marriage.

This chapter describes a step-by-step approach to building a relationship that has worked for thousands of men and women. It focuses on achieving your ultimate goal of dating—developing the building blocks for a healthy, satisfying marriage with someone who is right for you.

New daters find that this approach helps them date productively from the very start of their dating experience. Many long-time daters, some of whom insist, "I've been dating so long that I must know what I'm doing," have been able to make changes that helped them achieve what eluded them for so long.

We've broken the dating process into four stages—the first date, getting to know each other, developing emotional intimacy, and making the leap of faith.

STAGE 1: THE FIRST DATE

People often put so many expectations into their first meeting with someone new. You hope that you'll like the way your date looks, that you'll feel comfortable with him from the start, that your conversation will flow easily. You may expect to have a fun time together, to feel a strong connection right away, to get a sense that you've found "the One."

Some of these expectations seem pretty reasonable and some may seem overly ambitious, but all of them put a lot of pressure on a dater. You stand a better chance of having a successful first date if you view your first meeting as an opportunity to break the ice with a new person, and nothing more.

How do you measure the success of a first date? If, when it's finished, you can agree to go out with the other person again.

This may sound disappointing. Most people want a first date to go well enough to make them feel excited about going on a second date. But the first date is far too early to feel excited about your dating partner or to have any sense of what's going to happen next. A large percentage of successful matches get off to a slow start.

There are a lot of reasons for this. Many people need time to warm up to a new person, and their conversation doesn't flow at first. One of the daters could have had a bad day at work or school or not be feeling well, and that will affect how they interact on the date.

Sometimes the element of surprise plays a factor in how you react to a new dating partner. Often you expect your date to have a certain look or personality type that you gravitate to, and it may take you a while to let that expectation go when you meet someone who doesn't match it.

If you tell yourself that the first date is just an ice-breaker, are there any criteria you can use to decide whether or not to go on a second date? Yes—if the date is simply okay, or better than that, you should agree to go out again.

That doesn't mean saying yes to a second date with everyone. There are many good reasons why a second date is a bad idea. You may want very different things out of life from your date, or you may feel uncomfortable being with the other person. You may feel that you can never get used to your date's appearance, or see very clearly that he or she is very far from what you are looking for. You can reach these conclusions even though you thoroughly checked out the other person before agreeing to go out.

FIRST DATE DO'S AND DON'TS

- **"Airplane talk" is perfect first-date conversation.** Imagine yourself on a ten-hour flight from New York to Tel Aviv. The person next to you smiles and asks about the book you're reading. You start to talk to each other to be polite and pass the time. You're not going to reveal anything too deep about yourself, but there are things to talk about.

  Similarly, on a first date you can share an entertaining anecdote, talk about an interesting hobby, briefly describe your job, comment on your surroundings, play "Jewish geography," and not get into anything too deeply.

WHEN FLYING BETWEEN CITIES ON ONE OF OUR speaking tours, we overheard a conversation between the man and woman sitting behind us. "Oh, look, we're flying over some farms," the woman commented to her seatmate, a man about twenty years younger than she.

"You know," he said, "I grew up on a farm."

"What was it like?" she asked, and he started to describe his life as a child.

The two of us looked at each other and exclaimed, "Perfect first date conversation."

- **Be careful not to talk about deeply personal matters or emotions,** even if you feel very comfortable with the other person. One dater described to us how these premature revelations make her feel. "I'm so easy to talk to that men sometimes tell me their deepest, darkest secrets on our first date. It makes me very uncomfortable. I wonder what kind of person would bare his soul to someone he doesn't even know."

- **Come prepared** with some interesting stories or observations that can help conversation start moving.

- **Be patient.** It may take your date a little time to warm up. You can ask your date questions that start with *how*, *when*, or *why*, because most people will answer them with a few sentences instead of simply "yes" or "no."

- **Don't imagine how you could ever be married to your date.** It's scary to imagine being married to someone you've just met...who slurped their soup or has a funny laugh. These thoughts can keep you from wanting to get to know them better. Try pushing them aside and telling yourself, *I'm going to enjoy* *getting to know someone new.*

◆ **Focus on the moment.** A lot of people analyze their dates. *What did he mean by that statement? Did I just make a faux pas? What will he think of me?*

It's impossible to answer these questions because you don't know what someone you've just met is thinking or feeling. You're better off taking the conversation at face value, observing the ambiance and appreciating it, and paying attention to the experience without thinking about any deeper meanings.

STAGE 2: GETTING TO KNOW EACH OTHER

DINA AND EZRA CHOSE TO GO ON A SECOND date simply because they each thought the other one seemed nice. Neither of them expected this second date to be a turning point. They knew it would take time to build a connection.

Ezra wanted to make their date more interesting than simply sitting in a hotel lobby or taking a walk. After he and Dina met, they walked past a toy store and he suggested, "Let's go inside. I've been meaning to buy a backgammon set for a long time."

With his new purchase tucked under his arm, Ezra led Dina to a pleasant café, and they spent their evening playing backgammon, having coffee and cake, and talking.

Dina had decided she would give a purpose to each date. In the past, she'd spent too much time talking about trivia, and she could go on half a dozen dates with someone without learning much about him. Dina was thinking about switching jobs to something that interested her more than what she was doing. She decided to tell Ezra about the process she was going through, and ask him where he saw himself going in the next five years.

This conversation was more thought-provoking than Dina had anticipated, and she and Ezra switched to some lighter talk. Dina realized that she was starting to see a side of Ezra that she hadn't ever observed on a second date before and wanted to know more about him. Ezra also thought the date was interesting, and figured, "Okay, I could go out with this girl again."

A few days later, they met again. They both liked art, and they went to an exhibit Dina had heard about. They found themselves discussing their tastes in art and music as they commented on the pictures in the exhibit.

Ezra felt their conversation was moving a little more smoothly this time. He wanted to get to know Dina better. On the other hand, Dina was barely feeling a connection with Ezra. "Should I give it some more time?" she wondered. "Can I go on one more date?"

Dina and Ezra's approach can work for most people in this early stage of dating. They realized that they wouldn't form a strong connection this early in their dating. They talked about different aspects of their lives and interests on each date, but also made a conscious effort to have lighter conversation as well. Each date gave them an opportunity to see a different side of each other. After three dates, each one asked, "Can I give myself a little more time to build a connection to the person I'm dating?"

MAKING A CONNECTION

This connection may still take time to build, but most daters expect it to take root between the fourth and sixth date. Some people are willing to have a little more patience, particularly if their dating partner has a number of qualities they admire.

This is often a turning point for a relationship—one or both daters may decide against continuing because they aren't connecting, don't feel attracted, or realize that they want different things out of life. Or they can both see potential and decide to continue dating.

BY DATE NUMBER FOUR, GERSHON WAS PRETTY sure Mina was the woman he wanted to marry. After they had dinner together on Thursday, he asked her out for *motza'ei Shabbos*, and they went on a long picnic Sunday afternoon. Gershon asked Mina if she wanted to go to a lecture with him on Tuesday, and planned another dinner on Thursday. He felt as if he was on a cloud, and each date with Mina reinforced his belief that she was "the One."

Unfortunately, Mina didn't share Gershon's excitement. At first, she felt flattered that he wanted to see her so often. But by Tuesday night Mina felt emotionally and physically exhausted. She was nauseous even thinking about going out to dinner with Gershon in two days. She couldn't pinpoint anything that had gone wrong, but wondered how she could feel this way. Did this mean that things weren't working out between them?

JUMPING TO CONCLUSIONS

When a couple overdates, as Mina and Gershon were doing, one partner may not have enough downtime to process what they're going through. For most people, building a relationship that will lead to marriage is a very emotionally intense experience, and they often unconsciously sort through what they are thinking and feeling as they go through their school- or workday, run their lives, and sleep at night. If they date four, five, and sometimes even three times a week, the person who seemed so great at first may now make them feel anxious, nauseated, or overwhelmed.

> Mina listened to our suggestion that she and Gershon go out twice a week for a while. They talked briefly on the phone most of the days that they didn't see each other. Mina no longer felt as if she was in the middle of a whirlwind, and was able to enjoy her dates with Gershon much more now that she had some breathing space.
>
> Two months later, when she called to tell us that she and Gershon were engaged, she commented, "I can't believe I almost broke up with him because I didn't realize that I was feeling overwhelmed."

An unexpected change in the momentum of a courtship might also cause a dater to jump to the wrong conclusion.

> YUDI TELEPHONED US, CLOSE TO DESPAIR. "EVerything was going so well with me and Alyssa. I felt comfortable with her from the very first date, and I

thought we were having a good time together. But last night, date number six, was awful. We couldn't keep the conversation going, and I felt so down. I'm afraid I blew it, and now things are going to go downhill."

We reassured Yudi, "You can have a bad date or a difficult phone conversation, even after several good ones. It happens to a lot of people and it doesn't mean that your relationship is starting to deteriorate. Often when something like this happens it's because something else in your life is causing you stress or distracting you, like a cold coming on, job pressures, a family emergency, even upcoming *yamim tovim*. Can you think of something in your life that might have affected how you felt last night?"

"You know," said Yudi, "I had the worst week at work."

"That sounds like a really good reason for you not to be at your best on a date," we said. "The quality of a relationship isn't reflected in how you feel at a particular moment, but in how it develops over a period of time."

Yudi felt relieved. He called us back after his next date to report that he and Alyssa were back on track.

STAGE 3: BUILDING EMOTIONAL INTIMACY

While Yudi and Alyssa and Gershon and Mina were learning more about each other, they were also developing an essential element of relationships called *emotional intimacy.*

Emotional intimacy is a feeling of friendship and mutual caring, safety, and trust that deepens over time. It's a quality that encourages two people to share their ideas and feelings and to want to spend time together. It's the reason one partner will turn to the other for comfort or support when they're upset, and the other will want to provide that help. An emotionally intimate couple will look forward to doing nice things for each other, and often can't wait to see the other person's expression when they open an unexpected gift or are at the receiving end of a kind gesture.

ARI AND DALIA ARE NEWLY ENGAGED. WHEN they walked by a gift shop one evening, Dalia pointed out a beaded necklace in a window display and commented on how beautiful the beads were. The two of them laughed at the price tag, and Dalia said, "It almost belongs in a museum instead of around someone's neck."

Ari is an occupational therapist who often uses crafts to help his clients with motor skills. He sometimes shops at a craft store that sells many types of interesting beads, and decided to look there for some special beads Dalia would like. It meant a lot to him to be able to give Dalia a gift from his own hands, as well as from his heart.

How did Ari and Dalia get to this point? The key word is *time*.

Emotional intimacy takes time to develop. The evolution takes place as a couple shares thoughts, feelings, and ideas, and gradually reveals information to each other that they consider to be very personal.

Two people who sense an instant connection on their

first date don't have emotional intimacy. They may be able to relate to each other very easily, but they haven't developed a sense of deep friendship, a willingness to trust, and mutual caring. They won't feel comfortable turning to each other in a crisis, sharing or hearing an embarrassing secret, or going out of their way to help their partner.

It takes more than a handful of dates for most couples to develop a strong emotional connection. We've found that the majority of marriage-oriented dating couples need to date for a minimum of two dates a week for four to six weeks, with occasional telephone calls in between the dates, to solidify this aspect of their relationship. Many couples need more time, while a handful can reach this point with fewer dates.

Sometimes couples are encouraged to make a decision about engagement after fewer dates, but we believe that most people do best by dating long enough to feel a strong emotional connection before they get engaged. We'll explain why in chapter 5.

STAGE 4: MAKING THE LEAP OF FAITH

We're often asked if there is a test a dater can use to confirm that they are at the right point in a relationship to decide to get engaged. There are a number of building blocks for a successful marriage, many of which develop during the time that a man and woman are dating. They all have to be present before a couple decides to get engaged.

But there's also another, less tangible element in the process of deciding to marry another person. A man and woman can have all the essential ingredients for a successful marriage, but the recipe only comes together after their wedding. A couple has to make their marriage their priority, devote time and effort to nurturing it, and sift through the many different ways they can do that to find what works for them. Their marriage's success will depend on their commitment, their efforts, and the help of HaKadosh Baruch Hu. Many couples find that getting from "passing the test" to becoming engaged requires a leap of faith.

What is the test? How can two people make the leap of faith? We'll discuss this at length in chapter 5.

FIVE COMMON DATING MYTHS

Like urban legends, these sound like they make a lot of sense, but they're not true.

Myth #1: The smartest and prettiest women get married first.

A woman who is very accomplished or attractive may receive more dates than some of her friends, but that doesn't mean that she'll meet the right person sooner than anyone else.

Myth #2: If you date a long time, you must really know what you're doing.

Someone who has been dating a long time may feel that he's become an expert. However, if he's been dating so long without meeting the right person, it could be that his dating repertoire isn't that effective. He may benefit from learning different strategies.

Myth #3: If things don't click on the first date, we're probably not right for each other.

Relationships take time to develop. Many wonderful relationships start off with both daters feeling neutral about each other, and it takes a few more meetings for them to feel they're starting to connect. It's impossible for two people to know they're right for each other the first time they meet.

However, if you realize any of the following, it's a good indication that you aren't well-suited to each other:

- You want very different things out of life.
- You don't have compatible values and goals.
- You have a strong distaste for your date's personality or appearance.
- It is difficult for you to sit through the date because you're so different.

Myth #4: First impressions are always correct.

People aren't always themselves when they meet someone new. Someone who's slow to warm up might be more comfortable on a second or third meeting. Another person might be charming at first but over time reveal himself to be controlling, selfish, or rude. And then there are normal mistakes people make and feel embarrassed about later—putting their foot in their mouth, talking too quickly or too much, or trying too hard to impress the other person. Their real essence may take time to come through.

Myth #5: If we date longer, the qualities that bother me about the other person will work themselves out.

No courtship is completely smooth. However, when something bothers you about your date and you can't come to terms with it or work it out at an early point in the courtship, you probably won't be able to do so no matter how long you date each other. It can occur when the other person seems right in so many respects, except for this one issue. When the right person comes along, major issues will either not be present or will get resolved relatively soon, and the courtship will be much smoother (see chapter 9).

CHAPTER 5

THE LEAP OF FAITH

WE'VE ENCOUNTERED THE FOLLOWING SCENARIO more times than we can count:

I'VE BEEN GOING OUT WITH SOMEONE FOR A COUple of months and the relationship is getting serious. He's a wonderful person, even though he's not the kind of man of man I always thought I would marry. I was looking for someone more intellectual/athletic/tall/professional/outgoing/handsome. I like him and he really has wonderful qualities, but I want to make sure he's the right one. How will I know?"

Men who ask this question often get right to the point: "I'm dating this woman and I think she's 'the One.' How do I know for sure? Is there a test I can take?"

THE "PAIR" TEST

There is a test, but it's one you grade yourself. It's a reality check about whether your relationship has all of the qualities that form the foundation for a stable, healthy, fulfilling marriage. Here are the first questions to ask yourself after you've spent time getting to know each other and feel you can relate to each other:

- Is the person you are dating emotionally stable, flexible, and capable of being a good partner in a marriage?

- Are your worldviews and value systems compatible?

- Are your goals and expectations compatible? What about how you want to achieve them—are you both headed in the same general direction?

If you answer yes to each of these questions, you can go on to Part 2 of the test, which determines whether the two of you have developed certain qualities in your relationship. These qualities are easily remembered by the acronym PAIR, which stands for the following:

- **P**hysical attraction

- **A**dmiration, **A**cceptance, and **A**ffection

- Emotional **I**ntimacy

- Mutual **R**espect

Let's go through them one at a time.

P: PHYSICAL ATTRACTION

Two people contemplating marriage should certainly be attracted to each other. But people have different ideas of what that means. Some people expect to be swept off their feet or to experience fireworks. This is not the kind of physical attraction a couple needs for marriage. And this infatuation seldom lasts for longer than a few months.

Chaim's story illustrates how those feelings could be mistaken for the kind of attraction that's more enduring.

FROM THE MOMENT CHAIM MET ARIELLA, HE WAS certain he'd found "the One." She was tall and slim with long auburn hair and a wide, joyous smile, and he loved how she spoke.

Ariella came from a family of sports enthusiasts and was a natural athlete. Chaim enjoyed taking nature walks and going bowling with her. Ariella had great taste, and they liked the same music. They had a lot of fun on their dates, and Chaim couldn't get over how lucky he was to have met such a fantastic person.

Chaim and Ariella talked about their college studies and their day-to-day lives, their tastes and interests, and the steps each was taking to find a job after graduation. Chaim felt that the next step was engagement and marriage, and he asked Ariella what she wanted in her life for the long term.

Ariella's dreams focused on the city where she wanted to live, how she wanted to furnish her first apartment, and where she wanted to go on vacation. Chaim thought that Ariella hadn't understood what he meant and asked her if she'd ever thought about what she'd be like as a person in another five years. Ariella confided that she always felt uncomfortable about a small bump on her nose and wanted to get a nose job.

It took another few weeks before Chaim finally admitted that he and Ariella had been relating to each other on a superficial level, and even though he liked her company, he couldn't see her as a lifetime partner or the mother of his children.

Two people can initially feel a strong chemical pull toward each other even though they don't know very much about each other's interests, beliefs, and personalities. This won't last for the long term unless the couple can look beyond their strong attraction and begin to relate to each other on a deeper level. Many couples who experience intense chemistry at the start of their relationship later realize that they don't have compatible goals or values, don't like each other's personalities, or have trouble relating on a deep level.

The majority of dating couples don't feel the instant attraction that contemporary culture tells us we should expect will occur when we've found the right person to marry. Some daters will like their partner's appearance from the start and feel comfortable talking to them right away, but there won't be fireworks, a click, or any other immediate sense that this is "the One." Others may feel neutral or ambivalent about the other person's appearance and say their conversation was "just okay."

Ultimately, it doesn't matter what two people feel when they first meet. What's important is how they feel about each other as their dating progresses.

EVEN AFTER FIVE CHILDREN, LEAH LOOKS LIKE A petite china doll. Blond, blue-eyed, and dimpled, many people would agree that Leah is a pretty woman, and her husband, Yitz, numbers among them. But Yitz admits that the first time he met Leah, he was unimpressed with her looks.

"I went for darker coloring and strong features," Yitz explains. "When I met Leah, I was disappointed because she didn't have the look I wanted. But we had a nice time and I decided to go out with her again. I remember when it hit me… We were sitting in a café, drinking hot chocolate and reminiscing about the way each of our mothers made hot cocoa. I looked across the table and realized, 'You know, she really is very nice looking!'"

Yitz discovered that attraction can grow as two people get to know each other. Many people will say that their date's looks "grew on them." And often, a dater who has a strong preference for a particular look will be able to let that preference go once he feels he's connecting to someone on an emotional level. She can look at the other person with fresh eyes and open herself to the possibility of being physically attracted.

How strong should the attraction be? You should feel comfortable with the idea of being with the other person. Many men are attracted by visual images, and they will want to like a woman's overall appearance. Women tend to be stimulated by other factors—if they're comfortable with a man, they may focus on features they find appealing, such as his gentle smile or the warmth in his eyes, and feel attracted.

It usually doesn't matter how intense these feelings are as long as they are present. Keep in mind that it takes some people three, four, or even five dates to develop feelings of attraction for someone they at first felt neutral about.

A: ADMIRATION, ACCEPTANCE, AND AFFECTION

Have you ever heard a friend describe the person they're dating? "She's amazing" or "He's a great guy" indicate that your friend admires their dating partner. They might be thinking about his ability to learn, her ability to organize and complete projects, his work as a Hatzolah volunteer, the way she gets along with other people, or his ability to see the silver lining in an unpleasant situation.

Admiring another person means that you look up to him. You feel that she has special qualities that set her apart from other people. Mutual admiration grows into a belief that each member of the couple is cherished and important to the other's emotional well-being, and this enhances the nature of their relationship.

Acceptance is a willingness to appreciate the other person even though there are things about him that you don't like. It means that you don't have a hidden agenda to change him to become more in line with what you want yourself. It means that you're able to look beyond less-than-ideal circumstances that she cannot change or control, such as a difficult background, a medical issue, or something unpleasant in her past.

In order to be able to accept someone, you have to be able to see their imperfections. All of us have character flaws and make mistakes. Some daters are so happy to be in a relationship that they overlook negative qualities in their partner while they are dating. They don't realize that they will eventually have to acknowledge these qualities and decide if they are able to live with them.

DAVID WAS SMITTEN WITH AVIVA, THE SECOND girl he had ever dated. One day, he commented to his father, "Dad, do you think there are some people with no character flaws? The girl I'm dating is perfect!"

"David," said his father, "no one is perfect. If Aviva seems perfect to you, it means you haven't dated her long enough. Until you know that she's not perfect and can accept her with her imperfections, you shouldn't marry her."

After several more dates, David and Aviva had hit a difficult time in their relationship. David noticed that Aviva was reluctant to talk about things that upset or bothered her or any challenges she had encountered. She hinted that her life hadn't been smooth, but wouldn't answer David's questions about it. It took a while for David to realize that Aviva avoided deep discussions about topics that were uncomfortable for her.

"You're right, Dad," he admitted to his father. "I see now that no one is perfect."

In contemporary culture, many couples decide to get married because they're "in love" with each other. **Affection** is an essential ingredient in the recipe for marital success, but it is only one of many ingredients needed for a marriage to succeed.

What's the difference between the love you feel for your parents, your siblings, your pet, your best friend, and the person you're dating? Is giddiness and feeling head-over-heels a definition of love? Is the emotion before two people are married different than the love they have for each other afterward? Which one is real?

These questions are very confusing to a dater. However, we don't need to answer them in order to know if someone is right for us. The word *love* doesn't describe the emotion we need for marriage.

Instead, we should think in terms of liking someone a great deal, rather than being "in love" with them. A deep feeling of affection is a more accurate description of the feeling two people should have before they decide they're right for each other. You need to strongly like the other person, to value him as an important person to you, to want to spend time with him, to feel you will miss him if he is not part of your life, and to be excited about the idea of building a life together.

People often call us in the middle of a *shidduch* when they are feeling pressured to become engaged even though they don't feel affection for the person they're dating. They are reluctant to become engaged because they sense that something is missing, and they don't know whether to believe the reassurances they've been given that those feelings will come after they experience married life with their new spouse.

These instincts are right. The affection two people feel for each other does grow after marriage, but in our society it has to take root before the couple gets engaged.

If it hasn't developed in the time the man and woman are dating, it is unlikely to develop after the *chuppah*.

Many times, a couple that seems to have all of the qualities each other wants in a spouse will discover that they can't connect on an emotional level even after a number of dates. That's because in spite of being right for each other on paper, they're not right for each other in person.

I: EMOTIONAL INTIMACY

When a dating couple begins to feel that they are more comfortable with each other and that they are developing an emotional bond, they are nurturing the seeds of emotional intimacy. As this bond blossoms, both dating partners feel a sense of friendship, are willing to confide in each other, regard each other positively, feel concern for each other's well-being, and sense that they can trust each other.

Emotional intimacy is a different, deeper feeling than affection, and it takes longer to develop because it's built upon the experiences a couple shares. Two people who insist that they knew the minute they met each other that they had met their soul mate don't have emotional intimacy. They have chemistry, but intimacy needs to develop gradually.

Couples who feel this deep sense of friendship and connectivity should be able to relate to each other without any pretenses; discuss experiences, ideas, and feelings; empathize with one another; give encouragement and emotional support; and feel comfortable being themselves in each other's presence. They do things that make each other happy and want to be someone the other can turn to for empathy and emotional support.

Emotional intimacy is a state of being that couples must develop in order to have a good and close marriage. Yet emotional intimacy takes time to develop. There's no hard-and-fast rule for how long it should take for a man and woman to feel this deep connectivity. It depends on the personalities of the daters, how focused they are on moving the relationship forward, and a host of other factors that we'll discuss in chapter 6, "Identifying Obstacles."

Most couples in our society need a minimum of ten to twelve dates to develop enough of a connection to feel emotional intimacy. During this time, they're able to see different facets of each other's personality and ways of relating, which enables them to have a better picture of the person they may marry. This strengthens their fledgling emotional connection and allows them to reach the next step.

BUILDING THE LAYERS OF EMOTIONAL INTIMACY

Emotional intimacy is the glue that holds a couple together. But rather than being like a space-age superglue, which only needs a small drop to form a strong, enduring bond, the glue of emotional intimacy is layers thick. Some of these layers are formed during courtship, while others continue to form throughout a couple's marriage.

Here are some ways you can add layers of emotional intimacy:

- **Vary what you do on a date.** Some dates should be interactive ones, such as shopping together for a gift, volunteering for a *chesed* project, or engaging in an activity like hiking or boating. A couple should have at least one long date, and if possible should see each other with friends and family (although in some circles, this only happens when you're about to become engaged). These are all excellent ways to see different dimensions of each other's personalities and to stimulate deeper conversations.

- **Have fun together.** Sometimes daters are so focused on finding out information about each other that they lose sight of the fact that they also need to enjoy spending time together. Smiling, laughing, and relaxing together adds a special quality to a budding relationship.

- **Make each date purposeful** by discovering at least one new topic of information about each other during a portion of the date in which you discuss something serious.

- **Talk on the phone** on some of the days you don't see each other, even if it's just to say, "Hi, how are you?" or "I'm thinking about you," or to share something interesting, funny, or upsetting that happened that day.

- **Demonstrate thoughtfulness, kindness, and concern for each other.** This could be as simple as saving a newspaper article about a topic that interests your date, baking cookies, buying a small treat you know he likes, or offering to pick her up at the airport after a trip.

  During this stage of dating, a number of changes may

take place that let you know you're strengthening your emotional connection. You may become familiar with each other's quirks, pet peeves, and senses of humor and can often anticipate some of the ways your dating partner will react to different situations. The two of you may have "in jokes."

You feel comfortable turning to each other for advice, problem solving, or emotional support. You look forward to doing nice things for each other. If you have a disagreement, each of you will want to try to work it out. For those couples who are accustomed to a longer dater period, you're no longer asking or being asked out on a date, but instead are checking to see what each other's schedule is like to know when you can get together.

R: MUTUAL RESPECT

From the very first meeting, each member of the couple must feel that he or she is being treated with proper *derech eretz*. You should be able to show your dating partner consideration and compassion, even when you disagree about something, and you should feel your date views you with respect.

There is no room in any relationship for a superior attitude or disrespectful treatment. Sometimes one person will begin to demonstrate a lack of respect for the other after the couple has become more comfortable with each other and each feels less of a need to be on their best behavior. If you feel that the person you're dating looks down on you, or feel humiliated by the way he treats you, don't make excuses for him. There are no excuses when respect is not present.

Y OSEF AND ESTHER HAD BEEN DATING FOR SIX weeks and had started to speak about getting engaged. Since Esther was newly religious, her seminary teacher was concerned that the relationship had progressed rapidly for someone raised in a secular environment. She asked Esther to bring Yosef by so she could meet him.

Yosef was polite to the teacher, but he vocalized a number of criticisms about the way Esther dressed and how she should change. The teacher understood that Yosef didn't admire or respect Esther, though he professed to like her.

When Esther's teacher discussed her observation with her, Esther realized that she had the same concerns but had been reluctant to acknowledge them. It was painful to admit that Yosef wasn't the man for her, but Esther realized she deserved someone who looked up to her and treated her with respect.

A REAL LEAP OF FAITH

E ven when you have all the ingredients for a good marriage, it may still be frightening to take that step and become engaged. None of us knows what the future will bring, and this often makes us hesitant to move forward.

Keep in mind that every couple who becomes engaged faces the same reality. We all need to make a leap of faith that, with our own *hishtadlus* and the help of HaKadosh Baruch Hu, we will be able to build our *bayis ne'eman b'Yisrael* on the foundation we developed while we were dating.

Each person experiences the leap of faith in a different way. Some will jump right in, and for others it's much harder. The coming chapters will analyze why this is so.

ARE YOU RIGHT FOR EACH OTHER?

The "test" to see if you're right for each other includes:

- Having common goals and values
- A belief that the other person would make a good spouse
- Having developed the following qualities, which you can remember using the acronym PAIR:

    Physical Attraction
    Acceptance, **A**dmiration, **A**ffection
    Emotional **I**ntimacy
    Respect

Without these qualities in place, you're unlikely to have the ingredients necessary for a healthy marriage.

CHAPTER 6

IDENTIFYING OBSTACLES

THE TALMUD (*BAVA METZIA* 59A) OBSERVES, "IF your wife is short, bend down and listen to her whisper." Our Sages explain that a husband should go out of his way to obtain and act upon the advice of his wife in household matters. This indicates to us the emotional intimacy that should exist between a husband and wife. As discussed in the previous chapter, emotional intimacy is an essential ingredient of marriage, and it's one of the building blocks that must be present before a man and woman decide to marry.

While there is no set time frame for emotional intimacy to develop, most daters expect to feel they are becoming connected after they move beyond their first several dates. As they share information about their lives, families, and aspirations and develop a history of shared experiences, they begin to feel more comfortable opening up to each other. They begin discussing their feelings about certain aspects of their lives that they only share with someone they can trust, and they start to feel an attachment to each other.

Sometimes, though, it may take a couple a while to develop an emotional connection. Occasionally, daters don't have an emotional barrier to closeness, but need help developing the conversational skills that can bring their relationship to a deeper level. Other couples may find it difficult to establish a bond because one or both of them is afraid to develop a close emotional connection with another person.

ELLA WOULD DATE A MAN FOR SIX OR EIGHT WEEKS, then break up with him for a simplistic reason, such as "He's my height and I wanted someone taller," "He and I are not at the same place religiously," or "I don't like his profession." These might have been good reasons for Ella to stop dating early in her courtships, but using them justify a breakup after several weeks of dating was a sign that she was just looking for excuses. What was she running away from?

Reuven figured out Ella's problem after they'd been going out a few weeks. Each time he tried to ask her how she saw her life ten years down the road or her feelings about certain subjects, she changed the subject. Finally, Ella said, "You keep asking questions about things I don't want to talk about. Why can't we just relax and have a good time?"

Reuven realized that Ella couldn't do more than date on a superficial level. Consciously or unconsciously, she avoided emotional intimacy.

When Reuven told her that this was the reason that he was ending their courtship, Ella finally acknowledged that she had a problem.

Some people who have difficulty becoming emotionally intimate find themselves stuck at the most basic level of dating conversation. Their dating partner may comment, "I like going out with Oren, but I feel as though we've been on ten first dates. I know so little about him. How can I help him open up?" Other daters will say that they were able to develop their relationship to a certain point, and now feel as if they can't go any further. Or they may realize that they often use humor or sarcasm to avoid topics they're reluctant to discuss.

DIFFICULTY OPENING UP

There are many reasons why you may have difficulty opening up to your dating partner. You may be naturally shy or reserved and feel uncomfortable confiding in someone else. You may have had a bad experience in the past when someone betrayed your trust, or you may be reluctant to disclose something embarrassing from your past.

Think about the reasons why it may be difficult for you to open up to someone else. Write them down, wait a day or two, and review them. This may help you understand your concerns and think of ways to overcome them.

Many daters find that they don't know how to have a meaningful conversation with someone they're dating. By preparing topics to talk about and practicing or role-playing with a friend, someone who is a little nervous or shy can feel more confident and comfortable when they're on a date.

The following suggestions have helped many people open up to their dating partners:

- **Write down some aspects of your lifc that you'd like to talk about.** This could be a talent you have, something you enjoy doing in your spare time, why you decided to attend a particular yeshivah or seminary, or a person you admire. Think of all of the different ways you can talk about these subjects.

- **Start with baby steps.** Find a good friend who's willing to help you in role-playing exercises. Select a general subject to talk about and spend ten minutes acting out how this conversation might take place on a date. Describe how you feel and think about the topic. Ask and answer questions that begin with the words *who, what, when, where, why,* and *how.*

  A day or two later, think of something more personal to talk about, such as a hobby or an inspiring experience, and practice another conversation, making this one last fifteen to twenty minutes. These dry runs should make you feel more comfortable about talking to a date.

- **Before a date, think about something that happened during the course of your day or week that was unusual or thought-provoking.** Did it remind you of another experience, a person you know, an issue you've been mulling over in your mind? On the date, describe your experience, beginning with a description of what happened and how it made you feel. You can then comment on the thoughts and memories you associate with the event.

♦ **It may help to be in an environment that makes you feel comfortable and is conducive to serious conversation,** such as a botanical garden or a quiet coffee shop. Try discussing a topic that is a little deeper than what you usually talk about. After ten or fifteen minutes, you can segue into lighter subjects, or simply enjoy each other's company. If at any point the conversation becomes too difficult or painful for you, tell this to your dating partner and then change the subject.

♦ **Don't overdose on deeper conversations.** You may want to have a more light-hearted discussion on your next date, and in a week or so introduce another deeper subject you never shared before. If you repeat the same cycle another few times, you should find it easier to speak about experiences and feelings. You may also see your dating partner opening up about more of his experiences and feelings.

In time, this exchange of thoughts and feelings will become an essential part of your relationship. In other words, you will have the beginnings of an emotionally intimate connection.

FURTHER OBSTACLES TO EMOTIONAL INTIMACY

It would be nice to think that shyness and awkward feelings are the only obstacles to emotional intimacy, but there are other, more complex challenges that can arise. As we will see below, a person may associate emotion with negative experiences, have suffered from too little emotional intimacy in childhood, have received mixed messages, be burdened by guilt, suffer from an inability to trust, or have a limited emotional range.

ASSOCIATION WITH NEGATIVE EXPERIENCES

Some people are afraid of emotional intimacy because they associate self-expression with negative experiences. They may have grown up in homes in which they learned from family dynamics not to express their feelings.

AS A CHILD, CHAVA SAW HER MOTHER RESPOND to her father's volatile temper by retreating to her bedroom in tears, rather than asserting herself or trying to discuss what had happened once her husband calmed down. Chava was afraid to discuss her feelings with either of her parents. She found it difficult to talk about anything of substance with her father, because he would become angry if she disagreed with something he said, and her mother would begin to cry if Chava revealed how she felt about what happened in her home.

Chava learned that it wasn't safe to express her feelings, especially negative ones, because when she did one of her parents became angry or upset.

LITTLE EMOTIONAL INTIMACY IN CHILDHOOD

If you grew up in a home in which your parents were unable to express their emotions, you may not have learned to do so either. For example, some parents seldom demonstrate their affection for their children by saying "I love you" or by hugging and kissing their children. Most of their interactions may revolve around activities that need doing, such as, "You have a dentist appointment after school" or "Please pick up your clothes and put them away." There is little discussion of feelings; no one speaks about being upset, angry, hopeful.

In this type of family, children rarely learn to identify and acknowledge their own feelings, and as a result, they can't express them. If a child is able to identify and acknowledge her own emotions, she may not be able to express them because she believes it's inappropriate to do so.

VERED GREW UP IN A HOME THAT CAN BEST BE described as formal. Vered's mother dressed her children in beautiful clothes and insisted that the family's designer-decorated home always look just so. She expected her children to do well in school, avoid outbursts of temper, and choose well-mannered friends.

These expectations went largely unspoken, but the children understood what their mother wanted from them. Conversations between the children and their mother were usually limited to the newest fashions, school goings-on, career choices, and making the right *shidduch*. Their mother seldom gave them more than a perfunctory good-night kiss.

Vered compared her home to the boisterous,

slightly chaotic homes of some of her close friends and much preferred the latter. She grew up with the nagging thought that her mother treated her and her siblings this way because she didn't really love them.

Vered's maternal grandparents had survived the horrors of the Holocaust and had married several years after the war. When Vered was growing up, her grandmother never discussed her life prior to her marriage. Later in life, Vered's grandmother suddenly began to speak about the Gehinnom she had endured.

Vered's family was shocked to learn that Bubby had been married to someone else before Zeidy, and that her three little girls had been brutally murdered. When she remarried and was blessed with Vered's mother, Bubby was convinced that if she loved this little girl too much, she might lose her, too. She held herself back from hugging and kissing her daughter, and sang lullabies in an undertone only after her baby had fallen asleep.

Bubby had refused to talk about her childhood or her first marriage with her daughter because she was afraid to open up a wellspring of emotions. She had taught herself to suppress a great deal so that she could function.

As Vered absorbed this information, she realized that her grandmother's legacy had now been passed on to a third generation. Her mother was aloof and superficial because she had learned this behavior from her own mother, not because she didn't love her children. Vered decided to work on herself so that she wouldn't repeat this pattern when she became a parent.

MIXED MESSAGES

If your attempts to express yourself were discouraged when you were young, you may have learned to suppress your feelings and limit talking about yourself. Let's say a child observed his father reacting to something that angered him by yelling and becoming red in the face. Once the blowup is over, the father may turn to his son and calmly say, "Oh, I wasn't really angry. I didn't really yell." If this sort of interaction occurs frequently, the little boy may begin to doubt what he has seen and learn that he should deny his own feelings.

In another scenario, a boy is reprimanded each time he cries and learns to keep his feelings to himself. A little girl may be repeatedly ridiculed for wanting to grow up to be a fairy princess and decide that it's better to hide her hopes and ambitions from other people.

Someone who grows up with a father who struggles with depression or alcoholism may see their mother repeatedly excuse his behavior by saying, "Daddy is sick. We have to be quiet." When his parents refuse to acknowledge the problem, the child also learns to deny problems.

GUILT

Some people think they don't deserve to be happy because they feel guilty about something that has happened in their past. They may push away appropriate *shidduchim* or unconsciously sabotage a relationship that has potential because they feel unworthy or because they are reluctant to reveal something that makes them feel ashamed.

A *ba'alas teshuvah* who behaved immodestly before becoming observant, a young man who shoplifted as a teenager, and a young woman whose twin sister was killed in a car accident many years before could be burdened by guilt that keeps them from moving forward in a relationship. They need to learn how to address this guilt so that they can become emotionally close to the person they are dating.

INABILITY TO TRUST

Perhaps you experienced something in your past that caused you to feel hurt or betrayed, and you're reluctant to make yourself vulnerable to a similar experience. Your fiancé may have broken your engagement shortly before the wedding, a parent may have abandoned your family, or a close friend may have breached your confidence by revealing a humiliating secret to someone else. You may be so shattered by these experiences that you've built a wall to protect yourself from getting hurt again.

HELENA WAS CRAZY ABOUT BARRY, WHO WAS EVerything she had dreamed about. She was so anxious to please him that she did everything he wanted, dressing the way he liked, sharing his tastes, and always agreeing with him. Helena never told Barry how she felt, but instead reflected his feelings. After they became engaged, Helena agreed with Barry's wish to live in the city even though she hated city life, and she went along with all of his furniture choices, even though she preferred something else.

Helena's parents had divorced when she was small

and she desperately wanted to please Barry so that he would always want to be with her. She was afraid that if he knew what she was really like, he wouldn't love her.

Barry often asked Helena to tell him what she was thinking and told her that he felt he didn't really know her. Shortly before their wedding, Barry broke their engagement for precisely that reason. He told Helena that he could never know what she was really like because she couldn't open up to him.

Helena was heartbroken, but she came to realize that Barry was right. She needed to learn how to express herself to someone she cared about in order to have a close, honest relationship.

LIMITED EMOTIONAL RANGE

Occasionally, someone who is afraid to open up and become close to another person has grown up in a family in which the parents have an emotionally intimate marriage and are accustomed to expressing their feelings to each other and to their children. The parents have been able to provide for their children's material needs and are concerned for their emotional happiness and well-being, and the children feel secure and safe in their family. Nevertheless, a child growing up in such a nurturing family may have difficulty understanding or expressing her feelings for another reason.

AT TWENTY-SIX, ELISHEVA WAS A FORMER BAIS Yaakov girl who enjoyed her work as a music therapist and felt close to her family and friends. Elisheva's parents often expressed their love for each other and their children, and the family got along well.

However, Elisheva's parents gave their children another legacy, too. They were kind, generous people who felt that negative emotions, such as disappointment or anger, shouldn't be expressed, and Elisheva absorbed this message. When she and her siblings were small, her elderly, widowed great-uncle lived in their home for the last two years of his life. As his health deteriorated, Elisheva's mother would tend to him and her several small children, often getting by on two or three hours of sleep without complaining that she was exhausted or overwhelmed.

Elisheva was attractive and personable, and had many dates. Many of the men she dated liked her and wanted to become serious, and she often thought that a man she was dating was "good husband material" and a likeable person. She hoped that she could form a connection with several of these men, and after seven or eight dates would wonder why she didn't feel close to anyone. She continued to go out, hoping that on the next date she'd be able to feel a spark of emotion.

Elisheva's seminary principal, with whom she'd remained close, persuaded her to meet with a therapist to understand why she was having so much trouble moving forward with any of the men she dated. Elisheva reluctantly agreed, insisting that she didn't need a therapist—all she needed was "to meet the right guy."

In a way, Elisheva was right. She hadn't yet met her *zivug*. However, even if he would have come along at this point in her life, she wouldn't have known it. She saw most of her dates as "nice" and couldn't differentiate between them because she had never learned to recognize emotions other than happiness.

Growing up in an even-keeled household in which negative emotions were simply not expressed, Elisheva had learned to push any negative feelings aside and ignore them. She didn't even know how to recognize them.

Although most of us would like to have a more positive attitude toward our lives, it's normal to experience negative feelings at one time or another. If we can't recognize our different emotions, we're deprived of a full range of feelings and of understanding our reactions to different people. For example, if we don't sometimes experience sadness, we can't recognize how intense joy can be. If we don't allow ourselves to say, "This date bores me," or "I don't like the way he treated that person," we can't make a connection with someone whose personality suits us.

Elisheva asked her therapist, "How are you supposed to know the right man for you? They're all nice."

Elisheva could have made a workable match with many of the men she dated, but she would have been deprived of the range of feelings she now has in her happy marriage. Elisheva's therapist helped her recognize emotions that were deep inside her, and she realized it was possible to experience varied feelings in reaction to different experiences and people.

There are many ways to become more attuned to your emotions and to otherwise overcome obstacles to emotional intimacy. We'll discuss some of them in chapter 7, "Overcoming Fear."

TIPS ON EMOTIONAL INTIMACY

It's important to understand that feelings of friend-ship and trust take time to develop, and that it happens according to a different timetable in each relationship. If you have difficulty opening up or understanding/ex-pressing your feelings, the following may help:

- **Practice talking with a close friend** about topics that touch you personally, or expressing more of your thoughts and feelings during your discussions.

- **Don't get discouraged** if it's hard for you to open up at first—as you break down some of the barriers and practice new skills, it will become less difficult.

- If even this seems too intimidating, **keep reading**. The exercises in chapter 7 are designed to help you become more aware of your feelings and more capa-ble of expressing them.

- Sometimes two people are perfect for each other on paper, but the connection just doesn't develop. It may be that their relationship isn't supposed to come to-gether at this point in time or that they really aren't right for each other. Here is where a dating mentor can be helpful (see chapter 9). No couple should be pressured to go forward with an engagement if they haven't begun to develop emotional intimacy.

CHAPTER 7

OVERCOMING FEAR

AT THE END OF CHAPTER 6, WE EXPLAINED THAT Elisheva was able to learn to identify her feelings, understand the differences between them, and recognize where they came from. Once she was attuned to her feelings, she was able to relate better to the people she dated. Many daters struggle with the same challenges as Elisheva, while others are able to identify their feelings but either intentionally or unintentionally suppress them. All of this can serve as a deterrent in moving forward in the dating process. The exercises in this chapter can help you get past this hump.

If we don't understand what we're feeling, we may have difficulty opening up to someone we want to be close to. This chapter describes an exercise that can help you become more aware of the emotions you are feeling, give them descriptive names, and recognize them when you experience them in your daily life. With time, you'll learn how to describe how what you experience affects you so that both you and the person you're dating realize when you're happy, sad, worried, frightened, hopeful, annoyed, flattered, impressed...and what makes you feel that way.

If you feel overwhelmed by the scope of the exercise, we've also described a partialization technique that can help you break it down into smaller, more manageable segments. This technique is also useful as a tool to keep you from overthinking your dating experiences.

TAKING OUT YOUR FEELINGS

The following exercise can help you understand and identify your emotions so you can to learn how to express your feelings when you become serious with a dating partner.

STEP 1: RECORD

The essential tools for this exercise are a notebook and a pen or an electronic device that will be handy at all times. For the first week, record all the feelings you experience, whether they are emotions or sensory responses, during the course of a day. Start the exercise as soon as you can after you get up. The morning is the most conducive time to begin, since you can write down your feelings almost immediately, before you've had an opportunity to suppress them.

What sort of feelings should you write down? Begin

with the first things you sense and feel when you wake up—hunger, tiredness, depression, anxiety, excitement, thirst. As the day goes on, continue to record the feelings you experience—at meals, at work, on the bus, when meeting friends, when getting ready for bed. "These cornflakes are stale—I'm annoyed at my roommate for leaving the box open." "The bus is pretty empty this morning. I like having a seat to myself." "The sky looks beautiful today. I feel calm looking at it." "I'm angry that my boss gave me all this work." "Boy, am I famished!"

Perform this exercise for a week. The more you write, the easier it will become to recognize the emotions and sensory responses that you experience throughout your day.

After the first week, concentrate on writing down only your emotions, and not your sensory responses like hunger and physical discomfort. "I just missed the bus. This is so frustrating!" "I finally finished my project. What a relief!" "I went out for dinner with friends and really enjoyed myself. I feel so happy."

You can continue with this exercise for any length of time, from several days to a few weeks. When you feel comfortable jotting down your emotions several times a day, you're ready for the next phase of the exercise.

STEP 2: EXPLORE

Now it's time to take out your emotions and touch them. Identify an emotion. What is it? Anger? What happened to make you feel that way? Did another driver park in your assigned parking spot, making you search for one at the far end of the parking garage? Do you feel this emotion in any part of your body? Where? What does it feel like? Do you see red in front of your eyes?

Or is the feeling envy? What triggered it? Your friend just got engaged? Do you feel like yelling, "It's not fair!"? Do you feel like curdling inside? Where do you feel this emotion in your body?

Or is the emotion love? Did you just hold your newborn niece for the first time? What's it like? Where do you feel it in your body? Do you feel warmth, like your heart is glowing?

This can be a difficult exercise, because we're often not accustomed to looking at our feelings, identifying what triggered them, and recognizing that they stimulate a physical response. If at first you find it difficult to record your emotions, try just writing down your sensory responses.

For example, shortly after you wake up, you feel hungry. Why? Has it been a while since you've eaten? Were your hunger pangs stimulated when you walked by the French bakery and smelled their croissants coming out of the oven? What does being hungry feel like? Is there pain in the pit of your stomach? Are you lightheaded?

With time, this exercise will become easier. It's a bit like riding a bicycle. Do you remember when you first tried to pedal a bike without training wheels? Do you remember feeling terrified that you would fall, even though your mom or dad was holding onto the back of the bike? You wobbled as the bike slanted this way and that.

As you improved, your parent shouted encouragement: "You're doing just great! I barely had to hold on!"

When it seemed you could balance the bicycle independently, your parent let go, and you were riding on your own! The next time you got on a bicycle, riding was second nature to you.

Similarly, this exercise is difficult and frightening at first. Many of us wobble all over, finding it hard to write down everything we sense. We have to rely on a notebook and can't perform the exercise without it. Later, we "catch our balance" and are able to focus on emotions—anger, love, joy, disappointment. By looking at the notebook, we can see how far we've progressed—we've moved from painstakingly trying to recognize our feelings to readily identifying them, understanding how they affect us physically, and recognizing what triggered them. After a period of time, this process becomes second nature.

STEP 3: EXPRESS YOURSELF

The final step of this exercise, and the one that takes the longest for most people, is learning how to express your emotions. At first, you can express your feelings to the people with whom you feel most comfortable, such as family or close friends. "I'm upset. We said we would meet at five o'clock. I waited forty-five minutes, and you never called to say you weren't coming."

ELISHEVA FOUND THIS STEP EXTREMELY DIFFIcult. She felt that expressing negative feelings was something "nice" people didn't do, and she was afraid she would make others angry if she expressed any negativity.

Elisheva's roommate often stayed up late, and

Elisheva felt uncomfortable asking her to turn out the light because it kept her from sleeping well. It took Elisheva three weeks to work up enough courage to tell her roommate that she was bothered by her late-night studying.

Finally, she turned to her friend, smiled, and said, "Chana, I have trouble sleeping with the light on. Do you think we can have lights-out at eleven-thirty each night?"

Chana responded, "I had no idea I was disturbing you. Of course I can turn the light out by eleven-thirty." Elisheva was surprised it was so easy.

It can take a while to work up enough courage to express your feelings even to people you feel close to. After it becomes easier, you can learn to express feelings to those in a wider circle, such as coworkers, people with whom you come into casual contact during the day, like your seatmate on the bus or the dry cleaner, and, of course, the people you date.

Elisheva was reluctant to tell her dates that she didn't enjoy a particular activity and went along with whatever they suggested, ignoring her own discomfort. One day, she mustered up enough courage to tell a date, "I think it's too hot to go on an outdoor picnic today."

When he said, "You're right. Let's have lunch in a restaurant and then go to the Jewish Museum," Elisheva was surprised that he wasn't upset. His response was positive reinforcement for this exercise, even though neither of them realized it.

Once you have successfully assimilated the process of getting in touch with and expressing your feelings, you'll find it easier to determine how you feel about the person you're dating. When you start to feel comfortable with your dating partner, you'll feel less threatened about revealing information about yourself and listening to what your date tells you about himself. This is part of the natural process of getting to know each other.

As you learn more about each other's personalities, tastes, and life experiences, you'll be able to identify and differentiate new feelings you may have, both positive and negative. This process stimulates further growth for you and your relationship.

PARTIALIZATION

Many people are overwhelmed when they perform the exercise described in this chapter because they experience emotions they are unaccustomed to feeling. If you feel this way, you may benefit from a technique called "partialization," which helps us break down what we are feeling into smaller segments that we can analyze and assimilate.

Imagine yourself on an elevator that comes to a grinding halt between floors. You start to panic, perhaps feeling that the walls of the elevator will move inward to crush you. When the elevator starts again and stops at the next floor, you rush out, surprised that you are quivering and perspiring. Only now can you look back on what just happened.

Look again at what you experienced, step by step. When you first entered the elevator, you felt a small amount of nervousness as the door closed because you knew you were in a vehicle you couldn't control. Usually the trip is quick, and your fear has no opportunity to develop further. This time, though, when the elevator jerked to a stop and didn't move again, your fear started to grow. You thought, *What if the cable breaks?*

You imagined plummeting down the elevator shaft at an unchecked speed. Then you thought, *Nothing's breaking, but what if we don't move for hours?* You imagined the air getting thin. You noticed that the fan inside the elevator had stopped. Beads of sweat formed on your forehead.

You clutched your cell phone, wondering who you could call for help. *Will anyone respond to the bell I'm ringing? Will I sound foolish if I start to scream? Will the lights go out next?* You started to shake with fright, and the shaking didn't stop until you stumbled out of the elevator doors.

Once you break your experience into smaller segments, you can realize that it was much less frightening and overwhelming than you felt at the time. You're able to acknowledge that some of your thoughts were irrational, and they triggered strong emotions that were out of proportion to the danger of the situation. The next time you're in an elevator that stops between floors, you may be able to control your imagination and avoid feeling a sense of impending doom, so that your reaction to the situation will be more rational.

Use this same technique with the emotions you feel about others.

THE FIRST TIME TANYA MET RAFAEL, SHE IMMEDI-ately felt drawn to him. He had such deep blue eyes and the most adorable dimple when he smiled. Tanya had liked his voice over the telephone, but in person it was even warmer. He was so easy to talk to, and seemed fascinated by everything she had to say. She felt she was floating on air throughout that first date.

After Rafael said goodbye, Tanya was overcome with apprehension. All her other first dates had been so lukewarm, and this was a totally new experience for her. She had never felt such attraction to anyone before. She was confused by her strong reaction and afraid to go out with Rafael again.

By partializing her feelings, Tanya was able to understand that she'd had an intense reaction to a very charismatic man. She acknowledged that Rafael was very good looking, had a wonderful voice and an engaging smile, and she had felt very special walking next to him. After acknowledging this, Tanya was able to set her feelings about his looks and charm aside and review what she had been able to glean about his personality. Rafael had been attentive to her and listened to what she had to say. He had been pleasant to other people, and had seemed to enjoy her sense of humor. She liked all of these qualities.

Because Tanya was able to differentiate between the instant chemistry she felt when she first met Rafael and the feelings that were generated by his actions on their date, she decided that Rafael was worth knowing better as a person and that his good looks and charm were a lucky bonus.

REHASHING YOUR DATE

There's another time we can benefit from the partialization technique. Some of us become overwhelmed after the first few dates with someone we like. Even though it's early in the dating process, we can find ourselves moving from thinking, *I'm starting to like this person* to *Can I spend the rest of my life with him?*

This is premature, and it not only inhibits our ability to understand how we are feeling but can also make us reluctant to continue to develop the relationship. This is the last question, not the first, that someone who is dating should ask.

Some people want to think about their experience when they return home from a date. It's not a good idea to replay the entire date in your head and try to analyze what every word and action meant, as some people are inclined to do. Instead, try to think about how you generally feel about the person you are dating, rather than the emotions you felt at any particular moment when you were together.

Do you feel comfortable in each other's presence, and find that it has gotten easier to carry on a conversation? Have the two of you gotten a sense that you're starting to build a history of shared experiences? Do you have a relatively favorable impression of how your date acts towards you and others? Do you feel positively about the prospect of seeing him again?

These are appropriate feelings and observations for this early stage of dating and can allow you to slowly deepen your emotional connection to your dating partner. The two of you can begin to reveal more information about yourselves and talk about your thoughts and feelings concerning more significant topics.

Over the next several dates, you can begin to ask yourself questions like *Are we moving in similar directions? Do our goals seem compatible? Do I respect this person? Do I feel respected? What do I admire about him? Is there anything that bothers me, and if so how much? What else do I want to know about him?*

Even now, it's too early to ask, *Can I spend the rest of my life with the person I'm dating?*

If your answers indicate that you and your dating partner are becoming more emotionally connected, this means that you're in the process of developing emotional intimacy. The key here is to allow your connection to develop gradually and not to expect too much too soon.

TAKING A RISK

You may wonder if, as you reveal more about your thoughts, feelings, and life to someone else, you place yourself at risk of being hurt if the relationship doesn't work out. Unfortunately, this is a risk everyone has to take at one time or another. We have to make an emotional investment in a developing relationship so that we can figure out if it is right for us.

As you become more comfortable talking about your life, thoughts, and feelings, you may find that you are attracted to a wider range of people than you limited yourself to before you began to work on yourself. Some of them may be more suitable for you than the type of person you used to look for.

You'll also find that you feel differently about going on a date now that you feel more comfortable expressing yourself. You may discover that you can relate to your dating partners on a deeper level than you did at first. This may give you the impetus you need to continue learning about each other. If it turns out that you aren't right for each other, you may still come away with positive feelings, such as, *Even though he wasn't right for me, he was a very nice man and I enjoyed meeting him*; *I learned so much about myself from this experience, and I think it will help me when I do meet someone who is right for me*; or *Hindy is a really nice girl, and I think she'd be perfect for my roommate.*

A WORD ON PHYSICAL INTIMACY

As observant Jews, halachic considerations guide our belief that physical intimacy before marriage is inappropriate. This approach is borne out by sociological observations. When physical intimacy is introduced to a dating relationship, the couple's emotional intimacy stops developing. Instead of the couple working to develop the emotional closeness that they need in order to make a commitment to each other, the balance between the parties becomes skewed.

Sometimes a dater will hold back from developing emotional intimacy because they're concerned about physical intimacy once they are married. Their fear or anxiety about physical intimacy may result from lack of education about relations between a husband and wife, or because of a traumatic or difficult childhood experience.

Fortunately, there are resources that can help them overcome their fears so that they can look forward to marriage and have a relationship with their spouse that is rewarding in all respects. Many *chassan* and *kallah* teachers have been trained to teach future husbands and wives how to relate to each other physically and emotionally, in addition to teaching the laws of *taharas hamishpachah*. There are also a number of *frum* psychotherapists who have undergone special training and certifications to help men and women overcome their fears and anxieties about physical intimacy.

Nefesh International, an organization of Orthodox mental health professionals, can provide referrals of qualified therapists in this area (see appendix A for more information).

TAKING OUT YOUR FEELINGS

Consider the following as you proceed through this book:

- Many people decide to skip the "Taking Out Your Feelings and Touching Them" exercise. Not every dater needs to perform it in order to develop an emotional connection with a dating partner. However, if you believe you have obstacles to understanding and expressing your feelings, we encourage you to take the time to do this exercise when you go back over this book, chapter by chapter.

- If you're worried about risk taking, the exercises described above should help reduce this fear.

- The thought of physical intimacy can be frightening for *frum* singles. If you believe this applies to you, seek out a qualified professional (or well-trained *chassan* or *kallah* teacher) who can ease your concerns.

CHAPTER 8

REDUCING BAGGAGE

EACH OF US CARRIES AROUND A CERTAIN AMOUNT of emotional baggage—an imprint placed in our minds by one or more painful events or situations we have experienced. These imprints are often hidden in the background of our thoughts, but they do have an effect on us. They can cause us to react to certain situations with feelings of discomfort or anger, although we often can't recognize the reason we feel this way.

The imprint has such a strong effect on our thought processes and emotions that we may consciously or unconsciously prevent ourselves from moving forward in certain situations and achieving our goals. For example, we may sabotage an opportunity to obtain a raise at work or a promising social relationship.

JENNY'S FATHER DIED OF CANCER WHEN SHE WAS seventeen, but she was never able to speak with her mother, family, or friends about the intense grief and feelings of abandonment she experienced when he died. When Jenny entered college, she was still sad and confused about her loss, but thought she was able to reconcile her feelings when she became *frum* in her junior year.

Jenny graduated with high honors and is now on the editorial staff of a magazine. Although she is a talented writer and editor, she has stayed at the same entry-level position for four years. In addition, Jenny has never had a serious dating relationship and has never felt attracted to any of her dates.

Lately, Jenny has been thinking about why this is so, and she believes there is a connection between her difficulty in establishing a connection to any of the men she has dated and her father's death. But she doesn't know what the connection is, and she doesn't know how to deal with the impasse she has reached socially and professionally.

Jenny doesn't realize that the heavy baggage she carries—her failure to work through her feelings about her father's death—has affected more than her lack of success in *shidduchim*. Jenny unconsciously feels guilty about making her way in the world when her father isn't present to experience joy from her success. She has been holding back her talents and her ambition at work because she is uncomfortable achieving her goals when her father died before he could achieve his.

Socially, Jenny has found fault with every man she has dated and has used this as an excuse not to invest herself in building an emotional connection. She unconsciously fears that if she marries, her husband will die young and abandon her, just as her father did.

Jenny would greatly benefit from working with a therapist who can help her recognize the reasons her life has stagnated and guide her in working out her feelings of grief and loss that she has not been able to address for the past eight years.

Like Jenny, many people realize that they're stuck in their social lives, work, or interpersonal relationships but don't see the extent to which the baggage they are carrying around affects their lives. Some people go through their days feeling an underlying sense of frustration or sadness because their lives seem empty or inadequate. These feelings may not be due to external factors. Instead, the baggage they carry weighs them down to such an extent that they create a no-win situation for themselves.

RENA AND RACHEL ARE FRATERNAL TWINS. BOTH were bright and cute children, but somehow, as they were growing up, family members gave each of them a label. Rena was called "the pretty one," and Rachel was labeled "the smart one."

As they got older, Rachel was valedictorian of her class, attended an Ivy League college, and became a lawyer. She always felt comfortable about her appearance, knowing that while she was not a stunning beauty, she was slender and attractive.

Rena became prettier as she grew, but she was always self-conscious about her looks. She wouldn't leave home unless she looked just right and felt that people judged her by her appearance. She also felt as though she lived under her sister's shadow. Rachel always seemed to do better in school, make better career choices, and have friends who liked her for her personality and intelligence rather than her appearance.

Rena shied away from more academically challenging classes in high school and refused to apply to a highly selective college, even though her grades and SATs were almost as high as Rachel's. She graduated from college with honors but rationalized that this was because she had selected an easy major. Instead of pursuing a career that would encourage her to use her intelligence and education, Rena found a job that wasn't very interested or challenging.

When Rena dated, she was haunted by the belief that men liked her because she was pretty and personable but weren't interested in her abilities or opinions. She was afraid that intelligent and accomplished men would find her boring and uninspired.

Just as she set low sights for herself academically and professionally, Rena set low sights for a prospective spouse. She often wondered why Hashem had not blessed her with the same intelligence and sense of personal satisfaction that Rachel possessed.

Each person's reaction to life experiences is unique. Some people are able to move forward in their lives even though they have had a traumatic experience like the early death of a beloved parent. Others are positively affected by situations in which they find themselves, just as Rachel was encouraged by the fact that family members thought she was smart. Still others, like Rena, unconsciously burden themselves with a label placed upon them in early childhood.

If you're feeling a sense of frustration or sadness about your life, or realize you're stuck in terms of your career or social relationships, you can reap many benefits from a five-step process for reducing baggage.

FIVE STEPS TO REDUCE BAGGAGE
1. IDENTIFY THE BAGGAGE YOU CARRY

This isn't as simple as it sounds. Sometimes we don't even realize that we've carrying around an unresolved issue or have been affected by an experience in a way that interferes with our ability to deal with certain events or feelings in our lives. Other times, we may be able to point to a situation or event in our past that was particularly upsetting, such as the death of a close relative, a severe car accident, divorce in the family, or being bullied as a child. We may think we've dealt with it, but in reality, we haven't.

An upsetting situation may be hidden in your memory or may seem relatively minor, such as not being selected for a sports team or being rejected by a best friend in grade school, and you may not realize that it affects how you see yourself or interpret the actions of other people. All of these experiences have a common thread running through them. You've been changed by them, and that change affects how you think and feel about yourself and how you present yourself to the world.

MEIRA HAS NEVER FORGOTTEN A TRAUMATIC event she experienced as an eight-year-old child. After the incident, her forward-thinking parents brought her to a therapist who specialized in working with victims of abuse. Meira benefited from the therapy, and she would like to get married and have a family. However, now that she's dating, she's afraid that someone she likes may not want to marry her if he finds out what happened.

Meira's secret has become bigger than the actual incident, and she unconsciously says things to her dates to make them lose interest in her so she can avoid telling them what happened when she was young.

2. CONSIDER HOW IT HAS AFFECTED YOU

Once you've identified what has happened in your life that changed how you think about yourself, other people, or the world around you, you can move on to step 2: Recognize how your feelings about yourself and how you relate to the world have changed as a result of this experience.

SARA IS A SLENDER, ATTRACTIVE YOUNG WOMAN. When she was twelve, during a routine physical examination, her female pediatrician commented on the weight Sara had gained during a growth spurt and said, "You'll never get a husband like this."

At the time, Sara felt awkward about her changing appearance and, although she was not heavy, was deeply affected by her doctor's comments. Throughout adolescence, she felt overweight and unattractive, even though she was growing normally.

As an adult, Sara still feels self-conscious about her looks. Other people see her as a pretty woman, but lurking in Sara's subconscious is a fear that she is too heavy and that no one will want to marry her because of her appearance.

Doing this exercise, Sara realized that she is insecure about her looks and isn't able to trust her own judgment about her appearance. She spends a lot of time trying to find clothing that makes her look thin, and constantly seeks reassurance from her friends that she doesn't look "too fat."

3. RECOGNIZE THE EMOTIONS

When the experience happened, you may have felt shame, anger, guilt, betrayal, abandonment, or fear. You may be still carrying these emotions with you, and they are affecting your daily life.

WHEN FRANCINE, THE OLDEST OF THREE CHILdren, was an adolescent, her parents went through a turbulent time in their marriage. She once overheard an argument in which her mother angrily exclaimed to her father, "That's it! Our marriage is over. I'm only staying with you for the sake of our children. As soon as they're old enough, we're splitting up."

Francine's parents eventually reconciled their differences and they've had a happy and loving marriage for the past several years. Nevertheless, Francine subconsciously fears that her parents will break up, and she feels she must stay at home in order to keep their marriage together.

Sometimes, as you connect pieces of information about past experiences and the feelings, thoughts, and behaviors they generate, you can recognize the interconnection between them. This is the first step in working through your feelings and stopping the unproductive thoughts and actions they trigger.

4. TAKE ACTION

Recognizing the baggage isn't enough; now you need to bring your emotions out into the open and work them through. One way to do this is to reexperience these feelings instead of hiding them in your subconscious once again. You can mourn what you have lost, express your rage or anger, acknowledge your guilt, or admit the betrayal, shame, or humiliation you feel.

Many people find it helpful to write about the incident or situation that affected them, describing what it was like for them at the time as well as how it has impacted their life today. You may want to write a letter to the person or institution that caused your distress. This is a stream-of-consciousness experience—grammar and punctuation don't matter, because the purpose of this letter is to enable you to express yourself freely. When the letter is finished, you can either keep it or tear it up. It isn't intended to be sent.

You may find this part of the exercise to be very painful, and you would prefer to be guided through it by a therapist. A therapist may be able to help you use visualization techniques, similar to the ones we describe in chapter 10, to walk you through the incident and the feelings you experienced in its aftermath. A therapist may also be able to help you identify the unproductive thoughts those feelings generate, and understand why they are unhelpful, irrelevant, or irrational.

Therapy can take time, but it has helped many men and women move on in life. Someone we know once described her experience in therapy as "like peeling an onion. Each layer has to be carefully peeled away to get to the core."

AYELET, A VIVACIOUS TWENTY-ONE-YEAR-OLD, thinks she will never get married. She carries what she feels is a terrible secret—there is no *shalom bayis* in her home.

Ayelet's neighbors and friends think she has a wonderful family. Her well-to-do parents are active and respected in the community. They make a point of having a "date night" every week, and tell others this helps them appreciate each other.

However, inside their home, the atmosphere is very different. Ayelet's father is often overwhelmed by his responsibilities at work and for the community, and when he's stressed he lashes out at his wife and children. He yells at them at the slightest provocation, and insists that the house and family be run in a particular way. When he feels less pressure, Ayelet's father can be more flexible and calm, but no one knows what to expect when he comes home from work each evening.

Ayelet's mother retreats to her basement studio when he is in one of his moods. This is her way of keeping the peace, but the children still experience their father's volatility.

Ayelet doesn't know what she can expect from her own husband. She's afraid that a man who seems wonderful on the outside will turn out to be like her father, so she finds fault with every *shidduch*.

Ayelet feels that she cannot deal with the anguish and fear that she feels on her own. She needs the help of a third party, but is concerned because she'll have to discuss details about the behavior of other people. Ayelet can find the help she needs with a trained therapist who is professionally bound by an ethical responsibility of confidentiality. In addition, the family secrets she discusses with her therapist are exempt from the halachos of *lashon hara* (see Chafetz Chaim, *HaShiur HaYomi*, day 155, quoting *Chochmas Shlomo*, by Rabbi Shlomo Kluger).

5. FIND A NEW APPROACH

Now that you've identified and validated your feelings, you can find a new approach to help you move on. The purpose of this exercise is to help you move forward in your life and to release yourself from the pain you feel from your past. It's not an easy process, because many events can remind you of the pain you feel. You have to find an approach to life that will help you minimize the pain and keep it from blocking you.

VICKI HAS TAKEN EXTREME EFFORTS TO INSULATE herself from the pain she feels from an intense on-again, off-again relationship that ended in a last-minute broken engagement three years ago. Instead of dealing with her feelings, she forces herself to seem happy and vivacious. She pretends that she's much younger than her thirty-seven years, dressing in styles more appropriate for a twenty-year-old. Vicki forces herself to seem happy and light-hearted and makes many jokes, including self-deprecating ones. People who are close to her sense that her happiness is really the "tears of a clown" and that despite her efforts, Vicki is in a lot of pain.

Vicki decides to move to a new city, hoping to begin a new life and meet the right person. However, she doesn't take the time to plan the move by finding a job that reflects her skills and education. Instead, she accepts the first job offer she gets so that she can pay the rent, and plans to look for something better down the line. She finds a roommate whose lifestyle and personality are the opposite of her own, and the mix is volatile. Vicki tells herself all of this is temporary, because she'll soon find the right man to marry. However, she finds fault with every man she dates.

Vicki doesn't realize that she's unable to grow or move forward because she keeps running away from her painful feelings, instead of acknowledging them and finding a way to move past them.

You've taken the first steps that Vicki has avoided—identifying feelings and validating them. Your final step is to allow yourself to find more satisfaction and enjoyment in your life. Think of a child learning to walk—she takes small, unsure steps at first and has a hard time maintaining her balance. Still uncertain, she walks a little further, and as it becomes easier she can walk across the room.

You need to start slowly, too. Choose small activities that give you pleasure or accomplishments that allow you to feel a sense of satisfaction or competence. Later, when you feel more confident about yourself, you can expand the scope of your actions.

MICHELLE STRUGGLED WITH FEELINGS OF INFEriority for many years, and was keeping a journal of her progress as she tried to view herself as more capable. She wrote in her journal, "Today I did something I've never done before. I asked my boss for a raise. I was afraid he would get angry at me for asking, but I told myself that I've been working in this position for fourteen months, meet all of my deadlines, and have gotten mostly positive feedback. Even though I always second-guess myself, these are indications that I'm doing a good job, and I decided to ask for the raise in spite of my fears.

"Of course, I was anxious and had trouble sleeping the night before. I had practiced what I was going to say, but when I opened my mouth, the words came out differently. But I got them out and I sounded strong!

"My boss asked me how much of a raise I thought I deserved. Thanks goodness I thought that one through. I made myself ask for the five-percent raise I wanted, instead of giving in to the little voice that told me to ask for less. This was a big accomplishment for me. I was happy just to have gotten up the courage to ask for the raise, and I was assertive as well."

Michelle's request for a raise was one of a series of small steps she took over a period of several months. Some of them were scary, some were painful, and she could only accomplish some of them after giving herself encouragement and thinking of reasons why she should push past her fears.

You can follow Michelle's lead—setting a goal you believe you can accomplish, understanding and acknowledging the feelings you're experiencing, telling yourself why you can try for the goal in spite of your feelings, and congratulating yourself for taking the step. Celebrate each small accomplishment, and give yourself positive reinforcement for the next step you'll take.

ANOTHER HELPFUL TIP

Most people are aware of the health benefits that come from regular physical exercise. You may not know, though, that at least a half-hour of activity that raises your heart rate has a positive effect on your emotional health as well. Exercise makes our bodies produce endorphins, a hormone-like substance that helps elevate our mood and minimize physical pain. It also releases adrenaline, serotonin, and dopamine, which work together to give us a general feeling of well-being, help minimize depressed feelings, and help us feel more positive.

Vigorous exercises like walking, swimming, dancing, biking, and sports help stimulate your body to produce these beneficial chemicals. Find something you enjoy and make time to be active four or five times a week. You'll soon find yourself feeling and looking better, and it will be easier to meet the goals you've set for yourself.

A LIGHTER LOAD TO CARRY

People who have successfully performed the multilevel techniques for reducing baggage find that while they can't completely eradicate difficult experiences in their past, they can stop dwelling on the painful emotions and thoughts they generated. You may occasionally feel a twinge of discomfort or pain, but even people who aren't encumbered by excess baggage feel pain or discomfort from time to time. You've accomplished something very important—you're no longer stuck, and you've learned to move forward.

Compare this process to downsizing a duffel bag loaded down with a heavy stereo system. You want to listen to music, but the duffel is heavy and cumbersome. What if you replaced your stereo system with an MP3 player that you could carry easily in the palm of your hand?

It may take a few minutes to learn how to use your new device, but you'll only have a lightweight piece of equipment in your bag instead of an unwieldy set of speakers and a heavy disc player. You'll accomplish more than you ever did before because of the new tools and skills you've mastered.

SOME SIGNS THAT BAGGAGE IS WEIGHING YOU DOWN

- ◆ The thought of starting to date someone new makes you feel that you'd prefer to swim across the ocean or stay at home with a good book.

- ◆ You go on two or three dates and then realize that agreeing to a next date is a statement that says, "This is a possibility, and I'm interested." This scares you, so you start to look for reasons to say no.

- ◆ You can identify a specific pattern in a number of your courtships, such as being attracted to people who treat you badly or wanting to end the dating as soon as you sense that the other person likes you.

- ◆ You often experience a nagging fear that you won't make a good spouse.

- ◆ You worry that if the person you're dating gets to know you better, they'll lose interest.

- ◆ You won't allow yourself to get emotionally close to your dates because you're afraid things won't work out.

If any of these scenarios sound familiar, consider seeking help in overcoming these issues.

CHAPTER 9

HITTING AN IMPASSE

SOMETIMES A DATING COUPLE EXPERIENCES smooth sailing throughout their courtship and has an easy time deciding that they are right for each other. Others get off to a slow start, but gradually come to feel attraction and an emotional connection and in time realize that they have the ingredients necessary for a good marriage.

But many daters experience a bumpy ride to the *chuppah*. They may have to resolve interpersonal or cultural differences before they decide to move forward, or may need clarity to evaluate whether they're overlooking a genuine problem or overreacting to something that shouldn't be a concern. They may be unsure of their feelings, or may just need more time to process them. They may spend too long trying to make a relationship work when it won't, or need reassurance that reaching an impasse, having an argument, or feeling confused doesn't mean that a courtship won't work out in the long run.

This chapter gives you the tools to see your way through situations that aren't always easy to understand or evaluate.

HEAD VERSUS HEART

At times, you may find yourself at one place intellectually and at another place emotionally. Your intellectual side can apply logic and rational thought to a given situation, but your emotional side reacts to the situation differently because your feelings interfere with your thought processes.

IRA IS A LITIGATION ATTORNEY WHO KNOWS THAT his client's case can be settled easily because the other side has made an offer that's close to what his client is willing to accept. But Ira intensely dislikes the other attorney and allows his personal feelings to interfere with the settlement negotiations. He treats his adversary, who also believes the case can be settled, with such disdain that the lawyer now refuses to talk to Ira on the telephone, and the settlement negotiations collapse.

Ira doesn't realize that he hasn't been able to separate his feelings about the other lawyer from the thought processes he must use to settle the case. Instead, he blames the failure of settlement negotiations on the other side's stubbornness.

Like Ira, you may sometimes have difficulty separating your emotions from your rational thought processes in arenas such as school or work, where your personal feelings about a subject may interfere with completing the task at hand. The problem can be even more pronounced in the emotionally charged realm of interpersonal relations, particularly when it comes to dating. It's common for daters to feel confused or indecisive because the logical part of them tells them one thing, and the voice in their heart tells them something else. Yet thoughts and feelings both play an important role in building a relationship and deciding who to marry.

If you can recognize the dichotomy between your thoughts and your feelings, you can allow your head to work in conjunction with your heart.

A DATING MENTOR

Have you ever felt that you could really benefit from someone's experience and objectivity about dating? Most of your friends who are dating are as confused as you are. They might commiserate with you, but you feel you need more than that—someone who can see dating issues from a fresh perspective, because they've already been through it and aren't caught up in it. What you need is a dating mentor.

A dating mentor should be a happily married man or woman who has the discretion, life experience, and temperament to become a "go to" person for a dater who has questions about dating in general or about her current dating situation. Dating mentors serve as a sounding board, offer understanding and emotional support, and share suggestions about dating that are based on their perspective as a married person. A dater should be able to turn to a mentor before or after a date to either prepare for the date or discuss her concerns after the date is over. Most mentors provide encouragement for a dater who feels anxious or frustrated, a cheerleader when there is happy news, and a sounding board when a dater needs to vent.

A married friend or family member whose discretion and judgment you trust may be willing to mentor you. Or you may prefer to ask a current or former teacher or *rav*, or a neighbor or a friend's parent you feel close to. You may prefer to work with a professional dating mentor or coach.

TZIPPY HAD DATED THREE DIFFERENT YOUNG men before she met Shmuel. He was a refreshing change from her previous dating experiences. She'd agreed to go out on a second date with each of the three men, but those dates only confirmed her sense that the *shidduchim* weren't right for her. Shmuel, on the other hand, was articulate, pleasant, and attractive. Their *hashkafos* and family backgrounds were similar, and Shmuel had a good idea of what he wanted to do with his life. Tzippy enjoyed spending time with him.

After they'd been going out for a month and a half, Shmuel began to talk about marriage. Tzippy didn't feel ready to become engaged, but she didn't want to stop seeing Shmuel. She asked her older sister, Miri, what to do. Miri suggested that Tzippy find someone with more experience to talk to.

Tzippy lived next door to her former high school guidance counselor and felt that she was a good person to ask for advice. Mrs. Saffer was happy to be Tzippy's dating mentor and invited her to come over that evening to talk.

When Tzippy described what was going on between her and Shmuel, Mrs. Saffer pointed out that the two of them had seen each other only ten times over a period of six weeks. Even though Tzippy liked Shmuel, her feelings hadn't had time to catch up to the voice in her head that told her Shmuel possessed all the qualities of a good marriage partner. Mrs. Saffer explained that many times, one member of the couple gets to that point much earlier than the other, and that there was nothing "wrong" when that happened. She felt that Tzippy needed more time to get to know Shmuel better and decide if the positive feelings she had for Shmuel would develop into stronger feelings for him.

Since many couples in Tzippy's circles made decisions about engagement after ten or twelve dates, Tzippy spoke to her family's *rav* about needing a longer dating period, and he agreed with her. With Mrs. Saffer's encouragement, Tzippy told Shmuel that she was happy with the way their dating was progressing, but would be more comfortable if they dated a few weeks longer before talking about marriage. This longer dating period gave Tzippy time to appreciate Shmuel's good qualities and for her positive feelings for him to grow.

Tzippy and Shmuel have been happily married for more than ten years, and she so appreciated the help she got from Mrs. Saffer that she was inspired to become a mentor to two of her younger cousins.

Tzippy's situation was relatively easy to resolve. Her feelings hadn't moved as quickly as the timetable many *frum* dating couples follow. All Tzippy needed was time to allow her feelings for Shmuel to strengthen. Because she was permitted to take the time she needed, her emotions were able to catch up to her belief that Shmuel would be a good husband. A dating mentor helped Tzippy understand what her life experience couldn't provide.

DATING BURNOUT

Not all conflicts between head and heart resolve themselves as easily as Tzippy's.

TWENTY-NINE-YEAR-OLD RINAT HAD DATED many men since she began to go out at nineteen. She felt burned out and tired of the whole dating process. She'd had several first dates with men who appealed to her, but they weren't interested in going out again. Each time this scenario repeated itself, Rinat's self-esteem plummeted.

A *shadchan* arranged a date with Beryl, and both he and Rinat agreed to a second date. They went out a number of times. Beryl was thirty and it had taken him a few years of dating to decide that he was ready to settle down.

After a number of dates, Beryl asked Rinat to marry him. Rinat wasn't sure how to answe
r. She'd enjoyed going out with Beryl and thought he was a good, likeable man, but she wasn't sure if she

wanted to marry him. She told him that she needed more time, and he was understanding and patient. Yet this made Rinat anxious. Beryl was so attentive and caring, and she felt that he was trying to win her over. But she also worried that Beryl would wake up one morning and decide that he didn't want to marry her. She was so anxious she began to dread going out with him.

Rinat rationalized that she felt this way because Beryl was predictable and the time they spent together had become routine. She decided that the match wouldn't work out and broke up with him.

Rinat took a situation with strong potential and turned it into something negative because she was experiencing dating burnout. She understood intellectually that Beryl would be a good husband to her, and she even liked him. But she wasn't emotionally ready to allow her feelings for him to develop further. She'd become guarded because she'd been disappointed by other men who didn't want to give her a second chance. Each rejection had caused her pain, and she was afraid to trust that Beryl would continue to want her as his wife. She wouldn't allow herself to say yes to him and risk getting hurt again.

How should Rinat have handled her situation? Had she recognized the symptoms of emotional burnout, she might have realized that she needed a break from dating before she accepted a date with Beryl. Instead, she felt pressure to keep searching for Mr. Right, because she was, after all, twenty-nine and the "clocking is ticking."

A person who feels emotionally burned out desperately needs a vacation from dating. Just as you take a vacation from work or sometimes have a "mental health day" off to relieve yourself of job-related stress, a dating vacation will prevent you from feeling burned out by your *shidduch* experiences and allow you the space to think positively about dating again.

Some of the symptoms of emotional burnout include:

- Feeling demoralized or hopeless after a long period of unsuccessful dating

- A decreased self-esteem because of one or more negative dating experiences

- Reluctance to start dating again after the breakup of relationship that seemed to be heading toward engagement

- Feeling anger toward the opposite gender or the dating process

- Feeling overwhelmed by stress that's unrelated to dating (family illness, a high-pressure work project), but is so preoccupying that you have little interest in the success or failure of a *shidduch*

- Feeling unwilling, frustrated, angry, or hopeless at the thought of going on another date with anyone

It's virtually pointless to date when you're experiencing any of these feelings, because you have few emotional resources to develop a connection with someone else. Instead, if you recognize any symptoms of dating burnout in yourself, it's time to take a vacation that will renew your *neshamah* and rejuvenate your feelings of optimism.

A DATING VACATION

Think of a dating vacation as a time to regenerate, rather than as an abstention from social life. A co-worker who takes a much-needed break from a strenuous job might travel to a beach or ski resort, go on a cruise with friends, read a stack of bestsellers, or visit museums and attend concerts as a way of reviving her spirit and freeing her mind from the stresses of the workplace.

If you choose to take an intermission from dating, use it as an opportunity to do two or more of the following so that you, too, can simultaneously free yourself from the stresses of dating and nurture your soul:

♦ Find a form of regular exercise or physical activity that you enjoy, and do it three or four times a week for at least half an hour. Be creative and choose what appeals to you—Zumba, aerobics, spinning, Pilates, skating, swimming, running, team sports, using the machines at the health club, or a daily power walk with a friend. Aside from the benefits to your physical health, exercise helps you look better and feel more relaxed.

♦ Tap into the creative part of yourself by taking an art, music, acting, or dance workshop, or starting a craft project you've been meaning to make. Perhaps there's a gourmet cooking class calling your name, or an opportunity to learn guitar or piano. Whether it's taking a flower-arranging class, painting sets for a local theater production, or learning woodworking, almost everyone can find a creative outlet that appeals to them.

- Make a contribution to the community by organizing or participating in a *chesed* project, or begin attending a weekly *shiur* that interests you.

- Do something you've wanted to do for a long time, such as taking a trip with friends, going parasailing, or riding in a hot-air balloon. You can find one fun thing to do every Sunday during your vacation.

- Satisfy your intellectual curiosity by joining a book club, taking a course in medieval Jewish history, or learning a subject that has always seemed fascinating to you.

- Reconnect with good friends that you've been meaning to spend time with.

How long should this vacation last? Most people find that somewhere between six weeks and three months is good for them. During this time, it's important to remember that you're on a complete break from the dating process. If you took a vacation from workplace stress and spent every evening answering your boss's e-mails, it wouldn't be much of a rest, would it? Similarly, when you're on a dating vacation don't make plans for future dates, don't agonize over mistakes of the past, and don't even perform any of the exercises in this book.

You need to recover from an emotionally draining period of time by relaxing and focusing on a number of enjoyable activities, and you can't do that if you still have dating on your mind. If you're approached with a suggestion for a *shidduch*, you can explain that you're on a break for the next number of weeks and would welcome their suggestion after that time, if the other person is available.

BRACHA DECIDED IT WAS TIME TO TAKE A BREAK from dating when she realized that her last three dating partners all seemed to have the same face and that she wouldn't be able to recognize her Prince Charming if he rode up to her on his white horse. She realized she was feeling emotionally drained from a months-long series of dates with men who turned out to be poorly suited to her. Bracha told herself she would take three months off from dating, and tell anyone who approached her that she wanted to take a break until Rosh Chodesh Elul.

Bracha had always enjoyed acting and singing and had starred in many high school plays. She decided to audition for a women's musical production and won a part. She joined the swimming pool at the JCC and swam laps three times a week, a luxury she hadn't indulged in since she'd been in summer camp.

Bracha and three of her friends planned a week-long getaway at a relative's condo in the Berkshires. They enjoyed a restful Shabbos in the mountain air, a classical music concert, trips to the Clark and Norman Rockwell art museums, and touring small towns in the area. The price was right for their limited budgets, and they were only a few hours' drive from New York City.

As Rosh Chodesh Elul neared, Bracha realized that her vacation had more than served its purpose. She felt refreshed and ready to begin dating again, and was thrilled at how much she'd enjoyed herself over the summer. In addition, Bracha had rediscovered her love of acting and singing and realized that this could continue to be her creative outlet. She felt better about herself all around.

Most people return from their break from dating feeling emotionally replenished and better about themselves, and they are usually more optimistic about dating. If your dating vacation doesn't have the desired effect on you, it could be that your break was too short or that you didn't nurture your body, your creativity, and your need for relaxation and fun enough. However, if you followed our suggestions above and don't see any appreciable improvement in your emotional well-being, you may have to resolve issues other than burnout before you can move forward.

SPINNING YOUR WHEELS

Sometimes, both your head and your heart are trying to tell you something, but you have a hard time getting the message.

AKIVA AND TAMAR WERE SET UP BY MUTUAL friends, and their first few dates went very well. Akiva thought that Tamar was a very fine person, and he admired the fact that after she decided to become *frum* when she was twelve, she inspired the rest of her family to do the same. Akiva enjoyed dating Tamar and started to think that she might be the right one for him to marry.

Nevertheless, Akiva wanted to be sure. He had been in another relationship a year earlier when the woman he was dating decided to end things after they had begun talking about marriage. He took things slowly, telling himself that he needed several months to see if he and Tamar would be compatible in the long term.

Six months after Akiva and Tamar had started dating, they had met each other's parents and siblings, but were no closer to engagement than they had been three months earlier.

Akiva's parents sat down with him one evening to express their concern. "We see that you're still not sure what to do," his mother began. "It seems to us that you've reached an impasse, and if you stay stuck like this it's going to have a negative effect on your relationship. Tamar's a sweet girl, and we'd be happy to welcome her into the family, but we want you to do what you feel is right. We think you should talk to someone who can help you see your situation more clearly so you can make up your mind."

"You're right, Mom," Akiva said. "I am having trouble. Something's been bothering me since our third date, and I'm not even sure I can express what it is. I know it's not fair to Tamar. I have to come to a decision, but I don't know if I can be okay with what's bothering me."

"Akiva," his father said, "six months is a long time to keep dating when something is bothering you."

"Well, I hoped that after a while it would stop bothering me. I like Tamar and I think she'll be a good wife. That's why I'm still dating her."

With his parents' encouragement, Akiva decided to speak to a rebbe he had become close to while in yeshivah. Akiva explained that he was very uncomfortable with the fact that Tamar had low self-esteem, and constantly felt inferior to others. He wondered if his inability to accept this aspect of her personality was a good enough reason to decide not to marry her. His rebbe advised him not to get married if something about Tamar bothered him so deeply, no matter what it was. Akiva decided to tell Tamar that he had made a difficult decision to end their relationship.

Later, Akiva discussed his decision with his parents. His father said, "I didn't say anything earlier because I didn't want my opinion to influence your decision, but it's my belief that if you can't work out a major issue in the first few months of dating, you won't be able to do it even if you date longer. When you meet the right person, you won't have major bumps in the road like you had here. There will either be very small bumps or bigger ones that you can take care of quickly."

Less than a year later, Akiva met his future wife, and true to his father's predictions, there were no major bumps in their road to engagement and marriage.

Many people can identify with Akiva's experience. They date someone they believe is a good person who will be a good marriage partner, but something just isn't right. They may be very uncomfortable about a personality trait or something in their dating partner's background. Perhaps the couple has a major difference they can't reconcile, such as wanting to live in different countries, not being able to agree on the kind of education they want for their children, or whether they'll have a no-smoking policy in their home. Even though the dater can't come to terms with what bothers him or the couple can't find a mutually acceptable compromise of their difference, they keep on dating, hoping that in time they won't be bothered anymore or that a solution to their impasse will magically materialize.

This is like spinning a car's wheels when it's stuck in a snowdrift. Early on, with a little effort, we might have been able to get our car to move forward or backward. Now, though, the car's entrenched, and no matter how long or hard we try, we won't be able to get the wheels out of the rut.

The same thing usually happens when a dater can't come to terms with something that really bothers him or the couple can't resolve a major difference after many weeks of trying. They can continue to date, hoping things will work out, but they are really just wasting valuable time and setting themselves up for greater disappointment when one or both of them decides to end the relationship.

A DATING VACATION

Trying to figure out what to do on your "dating vacation"? Try some of these ideas, which have worked well for others:

- Sign up for a creative class—macramé, crocheting, painting, pottery making, sculpture.

- Learn to play the guitar, keyboard, or another music instrument.

- Love to read? Find a book club that meets every week or two and enjoy the selections it chooses.

- Does regular exercise sound boring? Try swimming, Zumba, handball, tap dancing, basketball, or martial arts.

- How about that trip you've wanted to take? Find one or more friends, pick a destination, call a travel agent, and plan an adventure.

- You can have a "stay-cation" even if you don't take time off from work. For the next month, set aside two or three evenings a week, and a Sunday or two, to explore interesting or fun attractions in and around your city.

- Take a spa day—many facilities have separate ones for men and women.

- Find a class or *shiur* on a topic you wouldn't ordinarily learn—*mussar*, an era in Jewish history, Malbim.

Most of all, enjoy yourself!

CHAPTER 10

VISUALIZATION TECHNIQUES

HAVE YOU READ THROUGH THE FIRST NINE CHAP-ters of this book and performed the exercises suggested, but are still feeling stuck? Maybe it's not a specific date that's troubling you, but rather your general aim and direction in life that's leading to confusion and uncertainty. You might benefit from trying a visualization technique that can help you get past the impasse.

Visualization techniques work by putting memories, ideas, and feelings into pictures. An idea or memory can become more vivid, and can open a flow of more memories, thoughts, and emotions. Many people find that as they process what they've experienced in a visualization exercise, they can see their situation more clearly. These techniques are often practiced with the assistance of a therapist, but we will describe two exercises that you can perform alone.

You'll be able to benefit from these exercises if you can be creative with your thoughts and if you aren't uncomfortable with the idea of reliving experiences in your past that may evoke discomfort or pain.

However, a note of caution: Some people find that these exercises are too difficult or painful to perform alone, and they need a therapist to guide them. If you're not accustomed to relaxing and letting your imagination flow, you may have difficulty performing either exercise without an experienced professional. In addition, if you've intentionally suppressed memories of past events, or if reminiscing is painful for you, don't try performing these exercises by yourself.

LOOKING INTO THE FUTURE

This technique operates on the old expression, "A picture is worth a thousand words." It is used to enable you to sort out some of your goals about your family life, determine if they're realistic, and identify any difficult emotions that may interfere with your goals.

The idea of this exercise is to picture your life in the future. While there are a number of settings against which you can project your thoughts, the setting we recommend is a Shabbos table—your own Shabbos table after you are married. This setting is significant because Shabbos is central to the spiritual and social lives of observant Jews, and because many single people base their opinions of married life on what they have observed at the Shabbos tables of their families and friends.

Before performing this exercise, make your environment conducive to a successful session. Make sure you have at least an hour to yourself, without the distractions of roommates, family members, telephone calls, or visitors. Take the telephone off the hook or turn off the ringer. Turn off your cell phone or put it on silent. Put a "do not disturb" sign on your door. Dim the lights and draw the blinds. Make yourself comfortable in a chair, on a sofa, or on a bed. You can perform this exercise either sitting or lying down.

Breathe deeply a few times. Give yourself a few minutes to relax from your everyday tensions. Then picture a Shabbos table headed by you and your future spouse. Visualize how the table is set—the Kiddush cup, dishes, cutlery, tablecloth, challah board. How is the dining room decorated? Is it a hodgepodge of relatives' gifts to a newlywed couple? Is it the tastefully furnished dining room of a more established family? Is the furniture modern? French provincial? Are those your grandmother's candlesticks on the sideboard?

Now look at your spouse and the others at the table. Do you have children? What are their ages and genders? How are they dressed? Are the children arguing? Do they look happy? What about you and your spouse? Is the husband making Kiddush? Is he leading the family in *zemiros*? Is anyone delivering a *d'var Torah*?

Do you have guests this Shabbos? Who are they? Are they relatives, friends, or both? What are they doing?

What is the topic of conversation? What are you/your spouse doing? Talking with guests and making them feel comfortable? Asking the children about their week? Giving your own *d'var Torah*?

What did you cook for Shabbos? Have you received compliments about the food you prepared? From whom? Who is helping serve and clear away the dishes?

Now imagine that your parents (even if they are not alive) are among the guests at the table. How do they interact with you, your spouse, and your children? How do they interact with your other guests? Are they smiling? Are they happy to be with you? Do you hear praise or criticism?

Now think about how you feel. Are you glad to be a host or hostess at your own Shabbos table? Are you apprehensive about your role? What other feelings emerge as you think about this future Shabbos? What are you afraid of? What are you happy about? Are you excited, content, angry?

Once you have finished going through these feelings, sit for a while and relax again. Then turn on the lights. Take some time to review the picture you envisioned. Identify the feelings this exercise engendered.

Do you think the picture you drew during this exercise was realistic? For example, you may realize that your vision of six spotlessly clean young children sitting politely at their places with hands folded while listening attentively to an adult's *d'var Torah* is a bit unrealistic compared to the slices of family life you've experienced at the homes of your friends. On the other hand, you may be very comfortable with your picture of yourself as an energetic young parent hosting your parents and next-door neighbors.

Was this exercise painful because it stirred up memories of conflict in other areas of your life? You may recognize that your jealousy of the attention to which your parents give your married sister and her children affects how you envision yourself as a married person as well as how you think about yourself now. Perhaps you need to work to unstick yourself from this unproductive focal point. If you're a *ba'al* or *ba'alas teshuvah*, you may be apprehensive about what it would be like to finally have a Shabbos table of your own. Does this apprehension project itself as feelings of inadequacy that you need to overcome?

Perhaps you long for the sense of comfort you feel when you picture your own home. How intense is your desire to fill your life with the rituals and symbols you missed experiencing during your childhood? Has it caused you to look for *shidduchim* who meet your idealized concept of a *frum* husband or wife rather than a partner who is better matched to you? Would introducing more rituals and symbols into your single lifestyle make you feel more fulfilled spiritually and enable you to better synthesize the qualities you seek in a spouse?

Was this exercise difficult for you because you continue to feel that you will never get married? Try to take a different approach to what you visualize. The results will be easier to accept.

S ANDY HAD TROUBLE VISUALIZING HERSELF AS A married woman. She was in her early thirties and repeatedly complained to her therapist that she was afraid that the time and money she had invested in therapy was wasted and that she would never be able to marry. Sandy's therapist recommended that she try this technique anyway and suggested that she imagine that she and her husband were hosts to a number of single adults.

This exercise helped Sandy move from her fixed focus on the present. She was able to visualize herself assuming the role of hostess that so many of her friends had played before, and this became a springboard to other projections about the husband and family she hoped to have.

If even after changing your approach you find it difficult to perform this exercise, or if after starting you find it either impossible to continue or too emotionally laden to handle, stop your efforts. Remember, this exercise is not for everyone.

REMEMBERING THE PAST

Sometimes a look into the past will give you new insight about yourself. People often don't realize the extent to which individual events in their lives have affected their emotional growth and personality. Even if you don't have heavy emotional baggage, there are still pivotal events in your life that helped shape your future. By taking the time to reflect on these events, you may be able to understand a little bit about why you act, think, or feel the way you do.

This exercise is intended to be an eye-opener. It is not a magical formula to change your life. However, after understanding more about yourself, you may decide to change your way of thinking about people or issues or how you act or react in certain situations.

Like the exercise described above, this visualization should be performed in a setting that is quiet, dimly lit, and free from all distractions. Once again, find a comfortable sitting or lying position. Close your eyes and take three or four slow, deep breaths and then begin to systematically relax your entire body.

Start with your toes. Wiggle them and then let them relax. Rotate your ankles and let them relax. Now move up to your legs. Pretend you can float and don't need to walk, and relax your legs. Go to your fingers. Wiggle them, and then let them go limp at your side. Think about your shoulders. Let go of the heavy burden you've been carrying and relax.

Move on to your neck. You need to release that tension. Move your head from side to side. Slowly relax your neck muscles. Imagine your head resting on a feathery pillow. Now allow your eyes to relax. Let your jaw go slack. Imagine that you are floating on a mattress of downy cloud.

Stay completely relaxed for a minute or two. While you are relaxed, think back to when you were a certain age — seven, nine, twelve, six. Now pick an event that occurred during that year. It could be the first day of school, a cousin's bar mitzvah, your birthday party, a school play, visiting day at camp, or some other day you remember. You can even select an ordinary school day, but choosing a particular day makes it easier for you to focus on the day's events.

Imagine waking up in the morning. Did someone awaken you? Who? Did the sound of the alarm rouse you? Picture yourself getting out of bed. Do you feel refreshed and ready to start the day? Do you stumble toward the bathroom? Are you grumpy, bored, excited? Now get dressed. Picture what you are wearing. Look in the mirror. What do you look like? Are you happy with your appearance?

Go to the breakfast table. Who's sitting with you? What are they eating? What are you eating? Was there a plate of steaming pancakes for everyone? Did you grab a few sips of juice and dash off to school? Did your mother have your place set with a bowl of your favorite cereal and a glass of juice?

Now picture yourself leaving the house to start your day (no sitting at home and reading a book in this picture). Where are you going? To school, to a party, on vacation? Are you alone? Are you with someone? Who? If you're in school, think about your teacher. What is she doing? Where are you sitting? What does the room look like? What's going on in class? At recess? What do you eat for lunch? Who do you sit with?

Who are your friends at school? Do you feel accepted, or are you snubbed by the popular crowd? After school, where do you go? To a friend's house? To a club or activity? Home? Who's with you?

What happens when you come home? Are your parents there to greet you? Do you come home to an empty house? Does your mom call from work to check up on you? Do you have to take care of your siblings? Do you eat dinner together as a family? Who cooks? Who sets the table? Who cleans up? What's on the menu?

What happens in the evening? Is there a bedtime story, homework and baths, learning together, games, or squabbling among the siblings?

Now it's time for bed. Do you feel you accomplished anything during the day? Was it a good day? Do you go to sleep tired and happy, or are you angry or anxious?

When you're finished picturing your day, take three or four deep breaths and slowly rouse yourself. Sit up and turn on a light. Review what you have remembered and how you felt about each scenario you envisioned.

Did you remember how embarrassed you were when you saw your bathing suit hanging on the lost-and-found rack at camp? Did you remember the stage fright that made you lose your dinner before the start of the high school play and how you overcame it after a few seconds in front of an audience? Did you remember cringing at the tension in your home when your brothers started punching each other and wrestling on the floor? Did you remember your father helping you with your math homework? Did you remember how you admired your new smile and chewed gum the day your braces came off?

Now think about how your memory makes you feel now. Does it make you smile? Does it make you angry? Can you say, "That was then, this is now, and I'm very different from who I was as a child"? Do you remember how much fun you had or how proud you felt about an accomplishment? After reminiscing about that awful toad costume you had to wear in the third grade class play, can you surmise, "Hey, that's why I never like wearing green"? Are you still upset about those painful experiences you had?

This exercise will stir up memories that can be pleasant, unpleasant, or a combination of the two. Some of them may enable you to see a connection between certain behaviors or attitudes you now exhibit and an event in your past. Even though you may not have to alter your behavior or attitudes, such self-awareness is always beneficial.

You may decide that you want to change certain patterns of behavior or thought. For example, this exercise may have helped you realize that you've made an incident in your past a focal point of your life and you haven't been able to move past it. You may be ready to address this issue in a manner that will enable you to unstick yourself and grow emotionally. Sometimes that can mean deciding to work with a therapist rather than trying to do this on your own.

ELENA IS A PRETTY, INTELLIGENT SPEECH THERA-pist whose friends and coworkers admire her for her graciousness as well as her sense of style. During high school, Elena blossomed from a gawky preteen who was always growing out of her clothes too quickly and seemed to trip over her own two feet. When Elena performed this exercise, she remembered the pain she suffered when she was repeatedly teased by her junior high school classmates.

"I realized that I still see myself as a gangly twelve-year-old with braces, and that this affects my sense of self-confidence whenever I date someone new."

Elena chose to work on her self-esteem with the help of a therapist.

Some people are able to use this exercise to make changes on their own.

DAVE IS A PERSONABLE THIRTY-THREE-YEAR-OLD who lives on the Upper West Side of Manhattan, which is heavily populated by religious single men and women. He is a financial analyst who earns a comfortable salary and rents an attractive apartment. Dave is part of a *chevrah* comprised of other religious singles from his neighborhood. He enjoys meeting friends for coffee and goes on many group dates. Weekends in the neighborhood have a Shabbaton atmosphere, and it is a must to have plans for *motza'ei Shabbos*.

After Dave visualized a day from his childhood, he started to think about other experiences in his life. He remembered how much he enjoyed his college days in New York. He'd always had friends around for a laugh, a pickup game of basketball, or a heart-to-heart talk. His current social life was very similar to the lifestyle he'd lived in college. Dave had loved college life so much that he wanted a part of it to continue for several years after he graduated.

Dave knew that it was time for him to move on and seek a serious one-on-one relationship with a woman, but he was afraid to significantly change the social life that gave him a sense of security. In addition, two of Dave's college friends had recently gotten divorced, and Dave admitted to himself that he was worried that divorce might someday happen to him as well.

Dave didn't change his lifestyle overnight.

However, the visualization helped him realize that his carefree habits and fears had kept him from growing up. Dave decided that his life was too self-centered, and that it was important to start thinking in terms of other people, leading him to volunteer as a Jewish big brother.

Dave made a further decision to stop living for the moment and focus on the future. He began to put more money into his savings plan at work so that he could buy a home of his own someday. He realized that if he continued to choose his dates with the same criteria he'd used in the past, it would be hard for him to find a marriage partner. Instead of simply dating a woman because she was fun to be with, Dave decided to look beyond this for the qualities he sought in a wife.

A VISUALIZATION OF THE FUTURE

People often use visualization techniques to feel more positive about achieving a goal they have set for themselves or to feel less anxious about an upcoming event or experience. Athletes, businesspeople, students, and actors report that when they envision themselves achieving a goal, they have a stronger belief in their ability and are able to focus on the steps they can take to attain what they strive for.

While we haven't focused on this aspect of visualization in this chapter, you can try this kind of visualization by closing your eyes and picturing a beautiful day in your life as a married person. Think of how it would be to wake up in the morning, married to someone you care about and who cares about you, and "walk" yourself through a glorious day of your *sheva berachos* week— preparing breakfast, talking, shopping for furnishings or groceries or opening some of your wedding gifts, having lunch, talking about the future, enjoying your evening with family or friends, and returning to your own home together, happy.

To help with your visualization, engage all of your senses. When you think about how everything will look, focus on colors, textures, light, and shadows. Imagine the smells—breakfast cooking, flowers on the table, perfume or aftershave you may be wearing. What are the sounds—music from the radio, laughter, birds chirping or traffic noises from outside your window, the joyful singing of the *sheva berachos* guests?

Can you taste the toothpaste on your toothbrush, the orange juice at breakfast, the trifle prepared for dessert? Don't forget about touch—the texture of the leather cover of your new siddur, the feel of the soap as you wash breakfast dishes, the sensation of wearing your new *sheitel* or hat, the fabric of your new clothes, the way your hand grasps the doorknob of your first home together.

Imagine the experience from your own eyes, pay attention to details, and take as much time as you like to dwell on them. This exercise may give you renewed hope and excitement in your search for your intended.

CHAPTER 11

WHEN YOU NEED A THERAPIST

THROUGHOUT THIS BOOK WE HAVE REFERRED TO situations in which an individual was able to resolve a difficult problem with the assistance of a therapist. Fortunately, we live in an age in which society understands and accepts that therapy can be beneficial to the average person who is having difficulty dealing with certain issues on their own. Both bright, personable individuals and quiet, more introspective personalities can benefit from one-on-one therapy sessions that help them identify and address issues that arise from past experiences and which they haven't been able to resolve or move beyond after a passage of time, which interfere with their achieving happiness, or which need to be put into perspective and integrated into a well-balanced life.

If you decide to work with a therapist, you will usually reap a double reward. Not only will you address the issues that affect you and work through them to achieve a healthier life, but also when you marry you will choose a spouse who is better suited to you than someone you might have chosen before therapy. This is because therapy has helped you understand yourself better, let go of emotional baggage that has weighed you down, and enabled you to see yourself more positively.

With this heightened self-esteem and self-awareness comes the clarity that can help you establish new priorities for the kind of life you want for yourself, as well as what kind of partner can help you build that life. It's similar to what someone with a vision problem does when they receive their first pair of eyeglasses.

Imagine you've been told that you need prescription lenses. You knew your vision wasn't perfect, but you're surprised by the difference once you place the new glasses on your face for the first time. You can't believe how different everything looks. Images are so much clearer and sharper. Details you previously couldn't distinguish are suddenly very prominent. For the first time, you can read the small print on the traffic signs, and you can see the beauty in each petal of the flowers growing in your neighbor's garden.

When you remove the glasses, you realize how blurred everything was in the past, and you are amazed that you didn't realize the extent to which your vision was impaired. Life is so much better now that you can see clearly.

Just as modern medicine has enabled us to maximize the gift of vision which Hashem has bestowed on us, it has enabled people to maximize His gift of human personality. If you find yourself in one of the following circumstances, we strongly recommend that you consider therapy with a trained mental health professional.

1. NOTHING HAS CHANGED

You've read this book and performed the suggested exercises and techniques as well as you can. Nevertheless, your dating situation has not appreciably changed. The people you date seem to be just like the ones you saw before you worked with this book, and you feel stuck and angry.

MOST PEOPLE WHO KNEW JESSIE, AN ATTRACtive and personable architect in her mid-thirties, couldn't understand why she hadn't married. She seemed like the type of woman most men would want to marry. However, over time, Jessie, who had always been optimistic and upbeat, gradually began to see herself as a loser.

Ever since graduate school, where she became observant, Jessie had never dated a man who felt serious about her. More than one date had expressed to friends that Jessie was too "good" for him. Recently, Todd had seemed like the right guy for Jessie. He was modern Orthodox, like her, and he enjoyed classical music and sports, just as she did. The two seemed to have a great time whenever they got together.

After dating for a few months, Jessie hinted that she and Todd might think about becoming serious with each other. Todd halted this conversation instantly.

"Remember what I said when we first started to date? I told you that I'm not ready to get married and I'm looking for someone I can enjoy spending time with, nothing more. Jessie, I like you a lot, but I'm still not ready to get married, and I don't see that happening any time soon."

Jessie was devastated. She'd believed that if Todd really liked her, he would change his mind. The couple agreed to split up, because Jessie wanted much more than Todd was willing to give.

In the aftermath of the breakup, Jessie bitterly admitted to herself that her breakup with Todd was similar to two other breakups in her recent past. Each man had warned her that he was not ready to settle down, and each time she had mistakenly convinced herself that if he fell in love with her, his attitude would change.

Jessie realized that somehow she was gravitating toward men who were simply not marriage material, and she needed help to understand why this was and how she could change her focus and, hopefully, her luck.

2. DISCOVERING UNRESOLVED FEELINGS

Perhaps you have unresolved feelings toward your parents that have prevented you from feeling comfortable about yourself and from entering or enjoying a serious relationship. You may be trying to find someone like one of your parents because you believe this is how you can "fix" your parent-child relationship. Or you could be finding it difficult to have a serious dating relationship because you feel angry or bitter toward a parent, don't trust members of the opposite gender, or worry that you won't know how to be a good spouse because your role models were so poor.

SHOSHIE IS THE ONLY DAUGHTER IN A FAMILY OF five boys. She always felt like Daddy's little girl and knew she had his ear—and his heart—whenever she wanted to speak with him. Of course, as the only daughter, Shoshie was a bit spoiled materially as well.

Shoshie's father died of a sudden heart attack when she was sixteen, devastating her entire family. Although Shoshie believes she has appropriately handled her grief, in fact she has been looking to replace her father through the men she has been dating. If a dating partner doesn't give her the same rapt attention and unconditional acceptance she received from her father, Shoshie leaves the relationship.

Ten years after her father's death, Shoshie still needs to address her relationship with her father and put it in the right perspective so she can search for a husband, rather than a substitute father.

ERICA'S WORKING-CLASS PARENTS MARRIED AT A young age, and their four children were born in quick succession. Her father was frustrated at the financial and emotional demands of his large, growing family. He resented the fact that he had dropped out of college in order to support his family and felt that he had grown old before his time. His bitterness manifested itself in his attitude toward his children. He frequently found fault with what they did, called them names, and put them down. Erica recalls constantly being told, "You're not worth the garbage I throw on the street."

Erica didn't start dating until she was in her early twenties. Even then, she found herself attracted to macho-type men who were underachievers like her father. Many of them were bitter and treated her disrespectfully. Erica rationalized that she deserved better treatment than she received from her dates, but deep inside she felt that what her father had said about her was true and that she was worthless.

Therapy enabled Erica to express her anger and shame about how her father had treated her, and she acknowledged all the pain she was carrying around inside her. She was able to understand that her father's barbs were not aimed at her personally, but were a result of his own inability to deal with his problems.

While Erica worked through her feelings in therapy, she experienced a number of small achievements in her professional life. She had started evening graduate school in accounting, she won a prize of an academic scholarship, and she received a promotion and a considerable raise at work. These small successes coalesced into a change in her self-esteem and her expectations for herself.

Erica found that she was becoming attracted to different types of men than those she had dated in the past. She is now happily married to a kind, soft-spoken man with whom she manages a successful *sefarim* and Judaica gift shop, and both of them thoroughly enjoy raising their three children.

3. DEALING WITH DIFFICULT EMOTIONS

The exercises suggested in this book are intended to evoke memories and produce emotional responses. Each exercise should be followed by a period of introspection that helps you better understand yourself or decide if you want to change some of your goals, priorities, ways of thinking, or responses to different situations.

Sometimes a person performing one or more of the exercises finds it difficult to deal with the emotions or memories that have surfaced. You may become preoccupied with a memory or emotion to the extent that it disrupts your daily routine, causes more anxiety than you're able to handle, or affects your sleeping patterns. Here's where a therapist can help you sort out your feelings and complete the process the exercises were designed for.

SUSAN, A GRAPHICS ARTIST AND DESIGNER, FOLlowed the exercise of remembering her past and imagined a school day from her childhood. She remembered that as she walked to school in the morning she saw her friends' mothers kiss and hug them as they went off for the day. How she longed for a kiss and hug from her own mother each morning!

Then she saw herself run in the front door after school, plop her books down, and look for her mother to share the great news—she had won the part she had wanted in the school play. Mom was in the den, sitting at a card table with three other ladies, playing mah-jongg. Susan felt that she couldn't share her news with her mother in front of the other women.

Later that evening, Mom was so busy preparing dinner and helping Susan's younger siblings with homework and bedtime that Susan felt pushed aside. At her own bedtime, Susan hoped for a kiss and a hug and a few minutes of quiet time together so the two of them could talk.

Her mother was reading while waiting for her husband to return home from a late night at work. Susan went over to hug her mother, who distractedly patted Susan's head and, still absorbed in her book, absently said, "Good night, honey," not even hearing the words Susan said to her.

Susan dejectedly walked off to bed, feeling empty and alone.

When Susan turned on the lights after the exercise was completed, a flood of memories poured forth. She remembered herself as an artistic and sensitive child who always felt neglected by her parents. Why hadn't they seen how much she longed for physical displays of affection and time for heart-to-heart talks? Why were they so busy with the day-to-day demands of caring for a family that they didn't have the time or the understanding to give her the attention she longed for? Susan cried herself to sleep that night.

For the next few days, Susan's thoughts were filled with memories of her childhood. She could almost taste the bitterness she felt. She found it difficult to sleep and couldn't concentrate on her work. Realizing that the exercise had touched a raw nerve that wasn't healing, Susan made an appointment with a therapist.

4. HEAVY BAGGAGE

Perhaps you recognize that you are weighed down with a considerable amount of baggage, and even after following the process described in chapter 8 you haven't been able to lighten that load. Alternatively, you may find yourself unable to confront the emotions generated by the baggage that has impeded your ability to move forward in life.

Most people with heavy baggage—certain issues or experiences in their past that have never been sufficiently resolved to enable them to move on emotionally—will need a therapist to help them address this impasse in a beneficial way.

5. DEPRESSION

It's natural for someone who feels frustration about dating and being single to have occasional twinges of sadness and concern about the future. But when that sadness turns to despair, or when a person exhibits signs of depression, it is time to seek professional assistance. Some of the more common signs of depression include the following:

◆ A sad mood for most of the day, over a period of two weeks or more

◆ A loss of interest in pleasurable activities such as eating, hobbies, time with friends, celebrations of *chagim*

◆ Changes in appetite (overeating or undereating)

◆ Insomnia or excessive sleeping almost every day; difficulty getting out of bed in the morning

◆ Frequently feeling physically agitated or moving as if in slow motion

- Frequently feeling fatigued or as if you don't have energy

- A pervasive feeling of hopelessness or worthlessness

- Difficulty thinking or concentrating at work, school, or home

- Recurring thoughts of suicide or death

Anyone who exhibits these symptoms should seek the help of a professional therapist as soon as possible. Depression can have a psychological and/or biological basis and can be successfully treated by therapy, medication, or a combination of the two.

6. ADVICE FROM A LOVED ONE

If one or more of your close friends or relatives are concerned about your welfare and recommend that you speak to someone, take their words into consideration. You may feel that your loved one is overreacting to your situation, and sometimes that's the case. However, if more than one person gives you this advice, or if it comes from someone whose judgment you trust, it may mean that you have an issue or problem that others have recognized and that you simply cannot see.

If you'd like to be able to understand yourself more clearly and address the issue you can't yet identify, a therapist can help.

WHY NOT A FRIEND?

You may wonder why you can't simply talk out your feelings with a close friend or a dating mentor whose advice you value. Many people find that their heart-to-heart conversations with friends help them put issues in perspective and assist them in working through areas that cause them concern.

However, if you fall within one of the categories described above, it's unlikely that you'll obtain the help you truly need from a friend, no matter how supportive that friend may be. Friends are not trained to handle an emotional crisis or clinical depression. Similarly, although they provide emotional support, friends are not trained in insight therapy, cognitive behavioral therapy, or other treatment methods that therapists successfully use.

Suppose you may harbor deep resentment toward a verbally abusive parent. Your friend may sympathize with and even agree with your assessment, but he or she will most likely not be able to help you acknowledge your anger, work through your feelings, and put them into a perspective that enables you to function better in life.

Most important, friends cannot always be objective. They may project their own opinions into your discussion: "I think you're crazy to take a painting class to 'return to your creative roots.' That's not practical. Why not join me at the karate class the community center is offering instead?" They may reinforce negative ideas that you are trying to overcome, saying, "Why shouldn't you want a husband who's going to make a lot of money?"

A friend may be disturbed if she learns that the picture she has formed of you is different from the person you really are. The new revelation may be unsettling. Alternatively, your friend, who truly believes that she wants only what's best for you, may be jealous of the progress you've made toward clarifying your goals and reassessing your priorities.

A therapist, who is an objective outside party and not involved in your personal life in anyway, can help you move forward without these biases.

SELECTING A THERAPIST

There are different types of therapists out there. Psychologists and social workers have been specially trained in a graduate-level program of psychology or social work to perform individual or group therapy. Psychiatrists are medical doctors who are also trained to perform therapy, as well as being licensed to prescribe medication when needed, often working in cooperation with a psychologist or clinical social worker in a combined program of therapy and medication.

Each therapist has developed a type of therapy that is unique to his or her personality and training. A person seeking a therapist can obtain recommendations from his personal physician or another medical professional, a well-respected friend who is knowledgeable about the mental health field, a congregational rabbi, or one's *mashgiach*, *rosh yeshivah*, rebbe, seminary teacher, or principal.

Should you limit your search for a therapist to one

who is Torah observant? Although there are varying approaches to this question, to us the choice is clear. Issues such as *negiah, tznius, taharas hamishpachah*, brief dating periods, and marriage at a young age are alien concepts to non-Jewish and most nonreligious therapists. When dealing with such topics as dating and marriage, which are intertwined with halachah and social norms unique to *frum* Jews, your therapy will be much more successful if the therapist understands and respects these concepts and does not have to be educated about them or convinced of their validity.

This is not to say, however, that there is no place for a nonobservant or non-Jewish therapist for Orthodox Jews. Any well-qualified therapist can successfully treat *frum* clients who suffer from mental illnesses and conditions, if this is what you are struggling with. Keep an open mind, and don't be afraid to keep looking until you find a therapist who seems to understand you.

It's important for a person to feel that they have a good working relationship with the therapist they select. If you're not comfortable with a therapist's personality, don't assume that therapy won't help you. This only means is that you and the therapist weren't a good match, and you may need to look further for a therapist whose personality and methods fit your disposition.

WHAT DOES A THERAPIST DO?

Most people who decide to work with a therapist want to lead happier and more functional lives.

Others come to therapy so that they can understand why they think and act the way they do. Often, a dater who has a good self-image and feels that most of her life is going well will choose to see a therapist because she believes something is blocking her from building a relationship that will lead to marriage.

A therapist should be able to help each of these clients identify feelings and unresolved issues. The therapist may have to help some clients uncover memories or feelings they've suppressed for many years or confront memories that often recur, and deal with them so they are no longer overwhelming, frightening, or crippling.

Some clients need a therapist's help to identify the emotions they're feeling and learn how to experience them. Still others will benefit from the therapist's abilities to help them improve their self-esteem, deal with excessive anxiety, learn healthy ways to interact with others, or learn better ways to evaluate different situations and react to them.

It's important to remember that in many cases, the goals of therapy cannot be accomplished in a few sessions. Many times, it will take time for the client to feel comfortable with the therapist and come to trust him or her, and only then will the client believe that he or she can be completely open in therapy. Furthermore, some issues are deep-seated or have caused years of pain, and it will take a while to explore their roots and resolve them. A client must be motivated enough to commit himself or herself to the entire process of therapy, even though parts of it may be painful or difficult.

Regular sessions will become just as important as

pursuing a degree or working at a job. They're not just opportunities to "talk things out" or a project that can be worked on "sometimes." If you feel that you need therapy, you'll have to be willing to put in this work, but in the long run, you'll be glad you did.

THERAPIST OR LIFE COACH?

If you feel you need help but don't see yourself fitting into any of the categories in this chapter, you might benefit from coaching rather than therapy. A trained coach who has obtained certification may help you:

◆ Acquire better clarity and focus

◆ Set life goals for yourself

◆ Establish an order of priorities

◆ Figure out a plan to achieve your goals

◆ Address issues you're challenged by in day-to-day life, such as time management or tackling necessary tasks you'd rather not do

◆ Improve your conversational skills

◆ Develop stronger socialization skills

◆ Become more proactive in your life in general, and in dating in particular

A number of individuals offer coaching services but have not been fully trained in the skills and standards of the coaching profession. We recommend using a life coach who is credentialed by the International Coaching Federation, a nonprofit organization that sets international standards for professional training, competence, and ethics, or who has been trained in a coaching school that is accredited by the ICF.

CHAPTER 12

LOOKING FORWARD

O UR GOAL IN WRITING THIS BOOK WAS TO HELP our readers develop an effective way to date for marriage—a way that would enable them to choose suitable people to date and to build a healthy relationship with someone who is right for them.

We hope that we have given you the tools to do that. We've discussed ways to acquire deeper self-awareness to and widen your choices about goals for yourself and your future. This knowledge will help you search for potential dates who best suit your disposition, needs, and goals.

We've given you an overview of the process of moving a first date through different stages of relationship building, and have provided a way for you to evaluate whether your relationship has the foundations for a rewarding and stable marriage. We've also identified difficulties many daters encounter and suggested ways you can try to resolve them—on your own, with the help of a mentor, or with the guidance of a therapist.

A word of caution: The advice in this book will only benefit you if you are sincerely motivated to find a spouse. It will not help you if you are going through the dating process because it is socially acceptable, because you want to satisfy your family's wishes, because your seminary teacher insists you should be searching for a husband, or because your rebbe has told you it is time to look for a wife.

This book won't inspire someone who isn't ready for marriage to change their mind or convince someone who's afraid of marriage to conquer their fear. If you're in either situation, we recommend that you not date at this time. As *frum* Jews, we are encouraged to date for *tachlis*, and you're not ready to do this. You can decide to work on getting yourself ready for marriage, or try to understand why you're afraid of marriage and address that fear. But until you do, why add unnecessary stress and disappointments to your life and the lives of the people you date?

JAY IS A THIRTY-FOUR-YEAR-OLD ORTHOPEDIST deluged with offers of "wonderful" *shidduchim*, but he's never been happy with any of the great women his friends and neighbors have introduced him to. He thanks them for their efforts and explains that he has high standards that are hard to satisfy. He feels that his standards are high because he doesn't want to worry about financial stability. Although he had a happy childhood, his family was very poor and both his parents struggled to provide for their children. Jay wanted to make sure that he'd be able to continue the long training for his specialty before marrying. He wanted his wife to have a good career or come from a well-off family, so that he wouldn't have to switch to a less challenging or lucrative specialty in order to support his family.

This rationale may have made sense when Jay was in medical school and completing his residency, but what happens once he joins a thriving medical practice? Now Jay feels torn between his expectation of finding a life partner, getting married, and raising a family, and the relief he'll feel if he pays off his medical school debts and stabilizes his position with his partners before he takes on more financial responsibilities.

In the interplay of conflicting emotions and rational thoughts, your emotions may say that you're not ready for marriage while your intellect tells you that Judaism encourages people to marry and have a close relationship with their spouse. Or, you could be like Jay and feel a conflict between wanting the emotional closeness of marriage and wanting to build financial stability—or any other goal—before you take that step.

If you are faced with this kind of internal conflict, parts of this book may help you examine and reassess your priorities and goals by looking within yourself. You may also benefit from speaking to a third party whose insight can help you clarity your goals. Only then will the rest of this book help you with the dating process.

May Hashem help you be successful in finding your *zivug* and in building a *bayis ne'eman b'Yisrael.*

BASIC DATING ETIQUETTE

FOR WOMEN

Here are some suggestions to help you make a good impression on the man you're dating:

◆ **Don't chase him.** Promising relationships can be cut short if a woman makes the man she's dating uncomfortable by pursuing him or prematurely expressing her feelings for him. When it comes to dating, men need to feel that they are the pursuer. That means that they do the asking out and they do the calling during the early and middle stages of a courtship.

◆ **Don't bring desperation and bitterness along on your date.** If you are angry, disappointed, or feeling desperate, you could inadvertently be projecting these feelings on your dates and scaring off someone who might be right for you.

◆ **Don't think of the date as being over before it's started.** You may have had a hard day and are in no mood to go out, but it's too late to ask to make it another evening. You've been able to talk yourself into things before, and you can talk yourself into this date, too. Take a quick rest, have a cup of coffee, freshen your look, and tell yourself that he may be a great person—if not for you, then for one of your friends.

◆ **Know how to end a date that's getting too long.** When a date seems to be going well, the man you're with may lose track of time. Or he may worry that if he ends the evening the wrong way, you'll get offended and not want to go out again. Or he may be enjoying himself, even though you don't feel the same way. It may be a good idea for you to diplomatically let him know that it's time to wrap things up. "I'm having a nice time, but it's already eleven-thirty, and I have to be up early tomorrow." Most men will get the hint and appreciate your diplomacy.

FOR MEN

Want to make a good impression on the woman you're with? Here are some suggestions to help your date realize that you're a genuine mensch:

◆ **Let her know the venue for your date.** That way, she can feel that she's dressed appropriately. If your date is inappropriately dressed for what you've planned, her level of discomfort may derail even the most promising *shidduch*.

◆ **Food is important.** It isn't a great idea to go out for a three-course meal on a first date—it's easier to break the ice with someone new in a less formal setting. But it's important to include some kind of refreshment on every date—either coffee, dessert, or drinks, or in the middle of your activity suggest, "Let's get something to drink/eat. What can I order for you?"

If you're planning to take her out for dinner, say so when you arrange the date, so she won't eat beforehand. And if your planned one-and-a-half-hour cocktail date turns into a long, animated conversation, be a gentleman and offer, "I can't believe how the time has flown. There's a nice café a few blocks from here—why don't we get something to eat?"

- **Your grooming's important, too.** After a long day at work or on *motza'ei Shabbos*, shower, shave, and wear fresh clothes. Your date will notice when you don't.

- **Do advance planning.** You'll make a good impression if you appear to have covered all of your bases. Know where you're going and how to get there. Carry enough money and credit cards so you don't have to stop at an ATM, and have an alternate plan in case the place you've selected has an unexpected closure. Don't keep her waiting in your car while you rush to daven *minchah*. And if you're planning to pick up your date and you don't have a car, it's a good idea to have a taxi wait at the curb while you go inside to meet her.

- **Always be a gentleman.** Okay, her looks aren't what you expected, or whatever you've been told about her is totally off. It's still important to be courteous and polite, and finish the date properly.

◆ **Make sure she gets home safely.** If you've picked her up, you're responsible to take her home, or at the very least to get her a taxi and pay for the fare. If you've arranged to meet, ask her how she's getting home. Take her to the bus or train stop and wait with her until it arrives. If it's late or public transportation is infrequent or far away, it's appropriate for you to drive her home or get her a cab.

◆ **Follow up with consideration.** If you don't think you're going to ask her date out again, just tell her, "It was very nice meeting you." Don't promise you'll call if you have no intention of doing so. Whether you want a second date or not, get back to the *shadchan* as quickly as possible. And if you're expected to arrange a second date directly, call your date within twenty-four hours.

RESOURCES

Chofetz Chaim Heritage Foundation
For information regarding *lashon hara* and *shidduchim:*
"When someone's life is in your hands."
1-800-867-2482

Dor Yesharim
Committee for Prevention of Jewish Genetic Diseases
In the United States: 718-384-6060
In Israel: 02-537-2111

Nefesh International
The International Network of Orthodox Mental Health
Professionals
201-384-0084
www.nefesh.org

Sasson V'Simcha—The Center for Jewish Marriage, Inc.
A nonprofit organization founded by the authors of this book to help Jewish men and women find the right person to marry and build a healthy, enduring relationship.
www.jewishdatingandmarriage.com

Shalom Task Force
Promoting Healthy Marriages and Peaceful Family Relationships
888-883-2323
www.shalomtaskforce.org

We encourage engaged couples to select *chassan* and *kallah* teachers who devote a significant portion of their classes to how a married couple can relate to each other on a personal level. In addition, we encourage all couples to participate in an early marriage education class, either during their engagement or soon after their wedding. Two fine programs are the Shalom Task Force's Shalom Workshop for engaged and newly married couples (www.chossonandkallah.com, 212-742-1141), and Bechirat HaLev in Israel (www.choiceoftheheart.org).

SUGGESTED READING

Einhorn, Rosie, and Sherry Zimmerman. *In The Beginning: How to Survive Your Engagement and Build a Great Marriage.* Southfield, MI: Targum Press, 2001.

Kramer, Shana. *Shidduchim 101.* Baltimore, MD: Make a Shidduch Foundation, 2008.

Levitan, Chana. *I Only Want to Get Married Once: Dating Secrets for Getting It Right the First Time.* Jerusalem: Gefen Publishing, 2010.

Manolson, Gila. *Choosing to Love: Building a Deep Relationship with the Right Person and with Yourself.* New York: Feldheim Publishers, 2010.

Manolson, Gila. *Head to Heart: What to Know Before Dating and Marriage.* Southfield, MI: Targum Press, 2002.

Ostrov, Shaya. *The Inner Circle: Seven Gates of Marriage.* New York: Feldheim Publishers, 2000.

NETWORKING VIA THE WEB

THERE ARE A NUMBER OF WEBSITES SPECIFICALLY geared for the *frum* community, and together they have helped thousands of men and women meet their spouses. This appendix will help you safely navigate these sites as well as offer guidelines on how to use them.

Virtually all networking sites offer an opportunity to screen user profiles while ensuring anonymity for both parties until they want to disclose personal details. Anonymity doesn't mean the same as security, however, and many sites advise users to conduct their own screening of potential dating partners.

Although many websites monitor some online activity or oust users who are found to be lying, all sites rely on the integrity of the users. This creates a golden opportunity for a con artist or otherwise unhealthy individual to log in and pretend to be someone he/she is not—and for individuals who are dissatisfied with their own reality to invent a new "Internet persona."

Despite its potential for abuse, online dating can be a helpful tool for introductions to other *frum* daters. If you use *frum* dating sites as a way to network rather than as a medium for conducting an extended online relationship, you may meet the right person. These guidelines can help maximize the benefits of using a *frum* website as a networking tool:

- **Start close to home.** The best way to start is by looking for potential dates within an easy-to-travel radius of your home. If you want to consider the profiles of people who live further away, be prepared to travel in order to date and be willing to relocate if things ultimately work out.

- **Arrange for a first meeting relatively soon after your initial online contacts.** If you like your e-friend's online persona and the references check out, it's a good idea to meet to see whether you're comfortable with each other's appearance and manner, and how each of you interact in person.

- **Don't date over the Internet.** If you engage in extended communication over the Internet, you may start to build a strong mental image of what your e-date is like. When you finally meet, you may be disappointed to find that the reality is very different from your mental image. If you meet before you develop this strong image, you will be more willing to get to know your e-date better.

Another reason to meet early in the process is that the person who seems so normal online may not be that way in person...or they may not actually want to meet because they can't handle a face-to-face relationship, or have lied about themselves and don't want you to discover the truth.

While the vast majority of people who use online dating services are well-adjusted adults, some are not. The potential to be hurt by someone you meet through the anonymity of the Internet is greater than if you are introduced by a mutual friend. Everyone who uses Internet dating should follow these simple precautions to help safeguard their privacy and keep out of trouble:

- **Keep it anonymous.** Most websites allow you to use a "display name" and to keep biographical details and contact information out of your profile. It's a good idea to remain cautious even after you decide to reveal your name and ask for personal references— don't disclose your home address, telephone number, e-mail, or where you work until you've had an opportunity to check someone out and then meet for the first time. Just because someone uses a *frum* website doesn't mean he's trustworthy or stable.

- **Arrange your first date for a public place, like a café or museum, and only after you've spoken with references.** Don't arrange to meet at your home or your office. At the end of date, don't travel alone in your date's car. Either let your date escort you part of the way home, or arrange for your own transportation. You are still relative strangers. Why put yourself in a situation that might prove dangerous or uncomfortable?

- **Keep an eye out for certain signs that the person you are dating may have problems** you'd rather not deal with, such as giving personal details that don't check out or behaving in a way that makes you wary or uncomfortable. Trust your instincts, and if your date seems too weird or scary, or you sense that you might be in danger, decide if you can politely end the date early, or just leave when you slip away to the restroom. It's better to be safe than sorry.

GLOSSARY

aliyah: Literally, "going up"; immigration to Israel or being called up to the reading of the Torah

ba'al/ba'alas chesed: A person possessing a generous, giving nature

ba'al/ba'alas teshuvah (pl. *ba'alei teshuvah*): An individual from a nonobservant background who has become religiously observant

bachur: A young man

Bais Yaakov: A school system for religious Jewish girls

bar mitzvah: Religious ceremony marking a boy's coming of age under Jewish law

baruch Hashem: Thank God

bashert (Yiddish): A person's predestined spouse

bayis ne'eman b'Yisrael: A Jewish home characterized by faithfulness and mitzvah observance

beis midrash: The study hall in a yeshivah

Bubby (Yiddish): Term of endearment for a grandmother

chagim: Jewish holidays

challah: Braided or round loaf of bread served at Sabbath and holiday meals

chassan (pl. *chassanim*): Groom

chavrusa: Study partner

chesed: Deeds of kindness

cheshbon hanefesh: Literally, "accounting of the soul"; taking stock of one's life

chevrah: Group of friends

chuppah: Marriage canopy

da'as Torah: The view of a rabbinic scholar

daf yomi: The daily study of a page of Talmud

daven (Yiddish): Pray

derech: Literally, "path"; the path of Torah observance

derech eretz: Literally, "the way of the land"; common courtesy towards fellow human beings

d'var Torah (pl. *divrei Torah*): Literally, "word of Torah"; a brief talk about a Torah topic

frum (Yiddish): Religiously observant

frumkeit (Yiddish): Religious observance

Gehinnom: Hell

HaKadosh Baruch Hu: Literally, "the Holy One, blessed is He"; a reverential way to refer to God

hakaras hatov: Literally, "recognition of the good"; gratitude

halachah (pl. halachos): Jewish law

halachic: Having to do with Jewish law

Hashem: Literally, "the Name"; a respectful way to refer to God

hashgachah peratis: Divine providence

hashkafah (pl. *hashkafos*): Religious philosophy integrated into one's lifestyle

hashkafic: Having to do with religious philosophy

hishtadlus: Personal efforts

im yirtzeh Hashem by you: God willing, it will also happen to you

kallah (pl. *kallos*): Bride

Kiddush: Blessing over wine or grape juice made at the start of a Sabbath or holiday meal

kiruv: Bringing other Jews closer to their heritage

klal Yisrael: The Jewish people

kollel: A post-graduate program of advanced Talmudic study in which most students are young married men

lashon hara: Literally, "evil talk"; malicious talk; gossip

mashgiach: A rabbi who supervises the emotional and spiritual well-being of students at a yeshivah

menschlichkeit: Common sense and sensibility

middos: Ethical values

minchah: Afternoon prayers

minyan: A quorum of ten Jewish males gathered for prayer

mitzvah: Torah commandment

motza'ei Shabbos: Saturday night

mussar: Moral teachings; a school of thought which emphasizes proper ethics

nebach: Unfortunate person

negiah: Literally, "contact"; a reference to the Jewish laws that restrict physical contact between men and women who are not married to each other

neshamah: Soul

parashah: A portion of the Torah

parnassah: Livelihood

rav (pl. *rabbanim*): Rabbi

rebbe: A rabbi who teaches in a yeshivah or seminary; a rabbi who is the head of any Chassidic sect; an instructor

rebbetzin: A woman who offers religious instruction; broadly, the wife of a rabbi

rechilus: Tale-bearing; gossip

Rosh Chodesh Elul: The first day of the Jewish month of Elul, which precedes the High Holidays of Rosh HaShanah and Yom Kippur

rosh yeshivah: A rabbi who is the dean or director of a yeshivah

seder: Literally, "order"; a set time for Torah study

sefer (pl. *sefarim*): Religious book

Shabbos: The Sabbath

shadchan (pl. *shadchanim*): Matchmaker

shalom bayis: Domestic tranquility

sheva berachos: The seven wedding blessings, repeated after the Grace after Meals at festivities that continue for the week after a couple is married

shidduch (pl. *shidduchim*): A matrimonial match

shiur (pl. *shiurim*): Class or lecture; class or lecture on Torah topics

shomer Shabbos: Sabbath observant

shul: Synagogue

simchah: Joyous or celebratory event

tachlis: A goal or goal-oriented; broadly refers to dating for marriage

taharas hamishpachah: Jewish laws of family purity

Talmud: The compilation of Jewish oral law given by God to the Jewish people, comprised of the Mishnah and the Gemara

tznius: Jewish standards of modesty
yamim tovim: Jewish holidays
yeshivah: An educational institution for Torah study
yeshivah bachur: An unmarried yeshivah student
yichus: A prestigious family background
Yiddishkeit (Yiddish): Jewishness; a halachic lifestyle
Zeidy: A term of endearment for a grandfather
zemiros: Special songs sung at the Sabbath table
zivug: Soul mate

ABOUT THE AUTHORS

Rosie Einhorn, L.C.S.W., a licensed psychotherapist, and Sherry Zimmerman, M.Sc., J.D., a psychotherapist and family lawyer, have worked extensively with singles in their private practices. They are the founders of Sasson V'Simcha—The Center for Jewish Marriage, Inc. (www.jewishdatingandmarriage. com), a nonprofit educational and advocacy organization dedicated to helping Jewish men and women meet, marry, and build happy, stable Jewish homes, and have developed and presented over 170 programs throughout North America, Europe, and Israel for single Jewish men and women and their communities.

Mrs. Einhorn and Mrs. Zimmerman are the authors of the popular books *Talking Tachlis: A Single's Strategy for Marriage* (Targum Press, 1998), which sold out four printings totaling over seven thousand copies, and *In The*

Beginning: How to Survive Your Engagement and Build a Great Marriage (Targum Press, 2001). They are chapter contributors to *A Practical Guide to Rabbinic Counseling* (Feldheim Publishers, 2005) and are featured presenters on the video-cassette series *Get the Ring: How to Find and Keep the Right One for Life* (Warm Wisdom Press, 2003). In addition, they write a weekly column, "A Dating Primer," for the *Jewish Press*. Their biweekly advice column, *Navigating the Dating Maze*, has appeared on Aish HaTorah's acclaimed website, www.aish.com, since the website's launch in 2000.

The authors have been interviewed and featured in Jewish radio and print media, including the *Jerusalem Post, Hadassah Magazine, Jewish Action, Family First,* the *Baltimore Jewish Times,* the *Jewish State, JM in the AM, Arutz Sheva Radio, Radio West,* and *Country Yossi.*

Mrs. Einhorn and Mrs. Zimmerman continually network with community leaders, rabbinic advisors, singles' organizations, matchmakers, and mental health professionals throughout the Jewish world to develop programs, materials, and resources that can better serve the single Jewish population. The organizations they have worked with on projects and programs include the Orthodox Union, National Council of Young Israel, Aish HaTorah, Jewish Learning Exchange, Chicago Community Kollel, Sasson V'Simcha Matchmating, Kol Simcha, Made in Heaven, United Synagogue, Jewish Learning Exchange, Saw You at Sinai, L'Chayim, and Nefesh International. They are presently developing a project with Yeshiva University's Center for the Jewish Future.

They may be reached at info@jewishdatingandmarriage.com.